D1553383

General Editors: J. R. MULRYNE
and J. C. BULMAN
Associate Editor: Margaret Shewring

King John

In this lucid and perceptive account of the text in performance, Geraldine Cousin argues that *King John* is a powerful play with particular relevance to our present-day world.

The book is primarily concerned with a director's and an actor's approach to *King John*. Attention is given to a number of key nineteenth-century productions, but the main focus in on twentieth-century perform-ance, in particular John Barton's two 1970s adaptations, the 1984 BBC television production and Deborah Warner's highly acclaimed 1988 RSC production.

This will be an invaluable book both to students of Shakespeare and to anyone interested in contemporary practical re-evaluations of a fascinating play.

Geraldine Cousin is Lecturer in Theatre Studies at the University of Warwick.

Already published in the series

Volumes on most other plays in preparation

Of related interest

King John

GERALDINE COUSIN

Manchester
University Press

Manchester and New York

Distributed exclusively in the USA and Canada by St. Martin's Press

Copyright © GERALDINE COUSIN 1994

Published by
Manchester University Press
Oxford Road, Manchester M13 9NR
and Room 400, 175 Fifth Avenue,
New York, NY 10010, USA

Distributed exclusively in the USA and Canada by
St. Martin's Press, Inc., 175 Fifth Avenue,
New York, NY 10010, USA

British Library Cataloguing-in-Publication Data
A catalogue record for this book is available
from the British Library

Library of Congress Cataloging-in-Publication Data
Cousin, Geraldine,
King John / Geraldine Cousin.
    p.   cm. — (Shakespeare in performance)
    Includes bibliographical references (p.)
    ISBN 0-7190-2753-5
    1. Shakespeare, William, 1564-1616. King John.
2. Shakespeare, William, 1564-1616—Stage history.
3. John, King of England, 1167-1216—In literature.
4. Kings and rulers in literature. I. Title. II. Series.
PR2818.C68   1994
822.3'3—dc20   93-49013

ISBN 0 7190 2753 5 *hardback*

Typeset by
Koinonia Limited, Manchester
Printed in Great Britain
by Biddles Limited, Guildford and King's Lynn

FOR MY PARENTS,
WINIFRED AND HERBERT

[v]

CONTENTS

*The illustrations appear between chapters V and VI,
pages 100 and 101*

[vii]

SERIES EDITORS' PREFACE

The study of Shakespeare's plays as scripts for performance in the theatre has grown in recent years to become a major interest for many university, college and secondary-school students and their teachers. The aim of the present series is to assist this study by describing how certain of Shakespeare's texts have been realised in production.

The series is not concerned to provide theatre histories. Rather, each contributor has selected a small number of productions of a particular play and studied them comparatively. The productions, often from different periods, countries and media, have been chosen because they are significant interpretations in their own right, but also because they represent something of the range and variety of possible interpretations of the play in hand. We hope that students and theatregoers, by reading these accounts of Shakespeare in performance, may enlarge their understanding of the text and begin, too, to appreciate some of the ways in which practical considerations influence the meanings a production incorporates: the stage the actor plays on, the acting company, the player's own physique and abilities, stage-design and theatre-tradition, as well as the political, social and economic conditions of performance and the expectations of a particular audience.

Any study of a Shakespeare text will reveal only a small proportion of the text's potential meaning. We hope that the effect of this series will be to encourage a kind of reading that is receptive to the ever-varying discoveries theatre interpretation provides.

J. R. Mulryne
J. C. Bulman
Margaret Shewring

PREFACE

In 1988 Deborah Warner directed an RSC production of *King John* which, in the opinion of many people who saw it, triumphantly vindicated the stageworthiness of an unjustly neglected text. Though there were a few dissenting voices, the majority of reviewers were extremely enthusiastic, Michael Coveney also commenting that it was the first time he had seen 'this tricky play taken seriously by the Royal Shakespeare Company' (*Financial Times*, 12 May 1988). For me, the experience of seeing the Warner *King John* was a major source of inspiration in the writing of this book.

'Tricky', however, *King John* undoubtedly is, for it is an elusive play in a number of ways. Its genesis is uncertain, its early stage history slender, and, though it achieved a considerable degree of popularity in the eighteenth and nineteenth centuries, it has since fallen into disfavour. Its precise subject matter is not easy to define, and, particularly in the twentieth century, theatre practitioners and Shakespearean scholars alike have complained of its incoherence and the difficulties presented by the singularly uncharismatic figure of John himself. There is also the problem that it is set in an age very distant from our own time, and that the small amount of information most audience members are likely to bring with them to a performance will be of little relevance. 'Everyone knows two things about King John', A. R. Braunmuller writes in his introduction to the Oxford Shakespeare edition of the play, 'he was Robin Hood's arch-enemy, and he granted Magna Carta.' Unfortunately, however, 'Neither the rural outlaw nor the legal document appears in Shakespeare's *King John*' (p. 38). The fact that there are unexplained gaps and inconsistencies in the chain of events, and that Shakespeare telescopes incidents from John's reign which in fact occurred over many years, does not help, though these are difficulties for the reader rather than for an audience caught up in the rapid forward momentum of the action.

As the title of this book makes evident, its concern is with *King John* in performance. *King John* is less well known than the majority of plays in the Shakespearean canon, however, and, for the benefit of readers who may find this background information helpful, the first chapter therefore outlines its stage history up until the end of the nineteenth century and discusses, in addition, twentieth-century critical responses to the play. Chapter II looks more fully at key nineteenth-century productions, while the remaining chapters all focus on twentieth-century performance. Chapter III deals chiefly with the 1953 Old Vic *King John* and the 1957 production at the Stratford Memorial Theatre, Chapter IV with John Barton's two 1970s adaptations of the play, the first at the Royal Shakespeare Theatre, Stratford-upon-Avon in 1974, the second at the Aldwych Theatre, London, in 1975. For both productions Barton drastically reworked Shakespeare's text, deleting many of the lines and inserting material from two other sixteenth-century plays about King John, in addition to dialogue of his own composition. His self-defined task was to provide *King John* with a coherence of perspective which, like a good number of other commentators on the play, he considered it lacked. His two versions of *King John*, therefore, present some similarities with Colley Cibber's early eighteenth-century adaptation which is discussed in Chapter I. The final chapters analyse two contrasting productions of the 1980s. The 1984 BBC television production forms the subject of Chapter V. Chapter VI is devoted to Deborah Warner's mould-breaking production which, I will argue, demonstrated both *King John*'s excellence as a play and its relevance to the late twentieth-century world.

ACKNOWLEDGEMENTS

With the exception of Chapter V, all quotations from Shakespeare's *King John* are from the New Penguin edition which was the version used in Deborah Warner's RSC production. In Chapter V, quotations from Shakespeare are taken from Peter Alexander's edition of the play (reprinted in *The BBC TV Shakespeare King John*), which was the version used in the television production. For the sake of clarity and simplicity, the spelling of characters' names has been standardised throughout the main body of the book, and follows the spelling in the New Penguin edition. Characters' names in the cast lists in the Appendix, however, conform to the spellings used in the original production. Quotations from the writings of Colley Cibber are from volume V of his *Dramatic Works* (AMS Press, Inc., New York, 1966). Quotations from *The Historical Register for the Year 1736* are from the Regents Restoration Drama Series edition. The photographs are reproduced by permission of the Shakespeare Birthplace Trust.

   I would like to express my gratitude to Deborah Warner, Nicholas Woodeson, Susan Engel and Antony Brown for talking to me about the 1988/89 RSC production of *King John*; Chris Parry for sending me details of the lighting for that production; Kate Brennan for her patience and skill in preparing the manuscript for this book; Ronnie Mulryne and James Bulman, the series editors, for their very helpful comments and suggestions; Michael Cooper for the enthusiasm he has shown for this project; and the staff of the Shakespeare Centre, Stratford-upon-Avon, for the invaluable research resources they provide.

[xi]

CHAPTER I

Introduction

King John in the sixteenth and seventeenth centuries

The few incontestable facts concerning the early history of *King John* are soon told: in 1598 it was listed among Shakespeare's 'tragedies' in Francis Meres's *Palladis Tamia*; it was initially published in the First Folio of 1623; the first production for which a record still exists was at Covent Garden in February 1737. Scholarly opinion is divided with regard to both the date of the play's composition and whether this precedes or antedates the publication, in 1591, of an anonymous play, *The Troublesome Reign of John, King of England*. Though the majority view has been that Shakespeare's play is a reworking of *The Troublesome Reign*, and must therefore have been written sometime between 1591 and 1598 (probably 1594–96), a number of critics, including recently L. A. Beaurline, editor of The New Cambridge Shakespeare *King John*, have argued that Shakespeare's play was written first, some time after the second edition of Holinshed's *Chronicles* in 1587. The argument in favour of the mid-1590s as the composition date rests chiefly on perceived similarities between *King John* and other Shakespearean plays of the period, notably *Richard II* (1595). Edmond Malone, writing in 1790, was the first person to point out the crucial importance of the year 1596 as a possible date of composition.

It is observable that [Shakespeare's] son, Hamnet, died in August, 1596. That a man of such sensibility, and of so amiable a disposition, should have lost his only son, who had attained the age of twelve years, without being greatly affected by it, will not be easily credited. The pathetick lamentations which he has written for Lady Constance on the death of Arthur may perhaps add some probability to the supposition that this tragedy was written at or soon after that period. (quoted in Scott and Williamson, *Shakespearean Criticism*, vol. 9, p. 218)

Whatever the precise year in which *King John* was written, and first performed, a contemporaneous audience would have found much in the play to relate to their own time. The prevailing fear of foreign invasion and civil unrest would have been only too well understood by an audience of Shakespeare's day. The internal strife which had torn England apart for so long had ended only with the accession to the throne of Henry VII, and though 'the great Armada of 1588' had been defeated, the country 'still faced the danger of an attack by a foreign Catholic power with support from Catholic dissidents within the kingdom' (Smallwood, New Penguin *King John*, p. 7). John himself, as Smallwood explains, had, with the Reformation, become the subject of a critical reappraisal, a new image of him 'as a Protestant martyr struggling against papal dominance' (*ibid.*, p. 10) superseding the wicked John of the old chronicles. It is in this guise, which casts him as a precursor of Henry VIII, that he is depicted in John Bale's fiercely anti-Catholic, mid-sixteenth-century play, *King Johan*. Here, John is a 'faithful Moses', Henry VIII the saviour who will eventually lead his people to 'the land of milk and honey'. *The Troublesome Reign* shares the anti-Catholic bias of *King Johan*, and, similarly, links John and Henry VIII, the dying John promising:

> From out these loins shall spring a kingly branch
> Whose arms shall reach unto the gates of Rome,
> And with his feet tread down the strumpet's pride.
>
> (II.1084–6)

Shakespeare's John is more complex – indeed, ambiguous – than his counterparts in the other two plays, but he too is

[2]

crucially related to the concerns of the sixteenth-century world. In various ways, he can be seen as analogous to Elizabeth I, who, like her father, was also in conflict with the Catholic Church. Both Elizabeth and John were viewed in some quarters as usurpers; both were faced with rival claimants to the throne (Mary, Queen of Scots and Prince Arthur); both, after the event, tried to distance themselves from responsibility for their rivals' deaths.

Though there is no record of the first performance of *King John*, it was presumably close to the date of the play's composition, sometime, therefore, in the 1590s. A number of possible allusions to lines in *King John* have been traced in plays of the period, and Beaurline notes that the role of Robert Faulconbridge, 'legs two such riding-rods . . ./ . . . arms such eel-skins stuffed', appears to have been 'written for a ridiculously skinny actor, John Sincler (Sinclo, Sinklo), who played bit parts 1590–1604 for Strange's, Pembroke's, and the Chamberlain's Men' (New Cambridge ed., p. 1). Evidence of a possible early seventeenth-century performance of the play, though, unfortunately, no date or other precise details, is provided by 'A list made on or about 12 January 1669 [which] allots certain plays, including *King John*, to Thomas Killigrew and the King's Company; the plays are described as "formerly acted at the Blackfriars and now allowed of to his Majesty's Servants"' (Braunmuller, Oxford Shakespeare ed., p. 81). If, as Braunmuller points out, '*King John* was in fact acted by the King's Men at the Blackfriars, then that performance must have taken place some time after the winter of 1609–10, when Shakespeare's company began acting there' (*ibid.*, pp. 81–2).

Eighteenth- and nineteenth-century adaptations

The first recorded production of *King John*, in 1737, took place in the context of Colley Cibber's attempt to stage his own drastically reworked version, *Papal Tyranny in the Reign of King John*, at Drury Lane Theatre. Like the best-known adaptors of Shakespearean texts before him – Davenant, Dryden, Nahum

[3]

Tate – Cibber attempted to prune and refashion Shakespeare's gifted, but, in his terms, chaotic, plays so that they were more in line with current aesthetic doctrine, chiefly the necessity that a play should be structured around the three unities – unity of time, unity of place and unity of action – and that tragedy and comedy should not be mixed.

By the time Cibber came to adapt *King John*, he already had one version of a Shakespearean text to his credit – though 'credit' is perhaps something of a misnomer in this context. In 1699 he had reworked *Richard III*, to include the admittedly stirring line: 'Off with his head! so much for Buckingham!' (an insertion which proved so popular that it was retained into the twentieth century, and was included in the Olivier film), and the woeful couplet: 'I'll climb betimes without remorse or dread / And my first steps shall be on *Henry's* head', which, far from climbing, sounds as if it is tumbling down a flight of stairs. It is difficult to imagine any actor, however talented, avoiding bathos with lines like that. In his dedication of *Papal Tyranny* to the Earl of Chesterfield, Cibber claimed that he had 'endeavour'd to make it more like a play than what [he had] found it in *Shakespeare*' (*Dramatic Works*, p. 242). The theatrical climate had changed somewhat, however, by the 1730s, and Cibber now found himself mocked for his arrogance in believing that he could improve on Shakespeare's original. While *Papal Tyranny* was in rehearsal, he wrote a piece in the *Daily Advertiser* (4 February 1737) attemptng to justify his adaptation by claiming that many of Shakespeare's plays had 'for these Hundred Years past . . . lain dormant, from, perhaps, a just Suspicion, that they were too weak, for a compleat Entertainment' (quoted in the Oxford ed., p. 88). The controversy, however, failed to die down, and Cibber 'one morning marched into Drury Lane Theatre, removed his script from the prompter's desk, tucked it under his arm and stalked out' (McClellan, *Whatever Happened to Shakespeare?*, p. 56).

When, on 26 February, *King John* was performed at Covent Garden, the publicity surrounding Cibber's abortive attempt to stage *Papal Tyranny* ensured a lively degree of public interest –

enhanced by the claim that the Covent Garden version 'As written by Shakespear' had the virtue of authenticity. In March, Henry Fielding's highly successful *The Historical Register for the Year 1736* was performed at the Little Theatre in the Haymarket. The action takes place in a playhouse and, when a character called Ground-Ivy, and who represents Colley Cibber, enters in the third act, the process of casting Shakespeare's *King John* is in progress. Ground-Ivy protests that '*King John* as now writ will not do', but, with a 'little . . . licking' by himself, it can be made serviceable. It is a maxim of his, he explains, 'that no play, though ever so good, would do without alteration. For instance, in the play before us the Bastard *Faulconbridge* is a most effeminate character, for which reason I would cut him out and put all his sentiments in the mouth of *Constance*, who is so much properer to speak them.' Medley, the author (in Fielding's play) of *The Historical Register*, aptly comments: 'as Shakespeare is already good enough for people of taste, he must be altered to the palates of those who have none; and if you will grant that, who can be properer to alter him for the worse?'

Papal Tyranny in the Reign of King John
When Cibber withdrew the play from rehearsal, it seemed that *Papal Tyranny* would be quietly forgotten. As Pope noted in the *Dunciad*, 'King John in silence modestly expires'. History, however, was to come to Cibber's aid, in the shape of a threatened Jacobite rebellion in the north of England and the consequent danger of a Catholic monarch on the throne. The staunchly Protestant Cibber had, as he explained in his dedication, been surprised that '*Shakespeare* should have taken no more fire' at 'the flaming contest between his insolent *Holiness* and *King John*'. How, he wondered, to account for Shakespeare's 'being so cold' in his depiction of this crucially important debate?

> Shall we suppose, that in those days, almost in the infancy of the reformation, when *Shakespeare* wrote, when the influence of the papal power had a stronger party left, than we have reason to believe is now subsisting among us; that this, I say, might make him cautious of offending? Or shall we go so far for an excuse, as to

[5]

conclude that *Shakespeare* was himself a Catholic? (*Dramatic Works*, pp. 240–1)

Cibber dismisses this suspicion as groundless, but identifies John's 'coldness' in his response to Pandulph as the springboard which impelled him to write his own play. It had been his intention to 'inspirit [Shakespeare's] King *John* with a resentment that justly might become an *English* monarch, and to paint the intoxicated tyranny of *Rome* in its proper colours' (*ibid.*, pp. 241–2).

On 15 February 1745 *Papal Tyranny* was performed at Covent Garden. The part of John was played by Quin, that of Constance by Mrs Pritchard. Colley Cibber was Pandulph. Two younger members of the Cibber family were also in the cast: Theophilus as the Dauphin and Jane as Prince Arthur. Sadly, at the age of seventy-three, Cibber had lost most of his teeth and could not enunciate clearly, so that in the large Covent Garden theatre a good deal of what he had to say was lost. Public response to the general acting style was also unfavourable, it being 'reported that the father had taught the son and all the rest of the persons in [the] play, the *good old manner of singing and quavering out their tragic notes*, and tho'' they spared the fault in the old man, they could not excuse the son' (Genest, *English Stage from the Restoration*, vol. IV, p. 162). Five days later, at Drury Lane Theatre, Garrick played John for the first time. Originally scheduled for an earlier date, the performance had been held over until after Cibber's benefit day. Mrs Cibber (interestingly enough, given the preponderance of Cibbers at Covent Garden) played Constance, Delane the Bastard, Macklin Pandulph and Miss Macklin Prince Arthur. During this season *Papal Tyranny* was performed a total of eleven times, and *King John* eight times. On six days the rival houses offered a choice of the two plays (Waith, 'Drama of history', p. 193).

Though it takes *King John* as its starting point, Cibber's play is very different. Few of Shakespeare's lines remain intact, even the haunting: 'Grief fills the room up of my absent child' being replaced by the infinitely more leaden: 'I have no son, grief now supplies his room'. The character of Constance is considerably extended, that of the Bastard drastically reduced. The whole of Shakespeare's Act I is omitted, so that John's defiance of Chatillon, the French Ambassador, his arbitration of the dispute between the Faulconbridge brothers, Philip Faulconbridge's (the Bastard's) decision to give up his claim to his inheritance and follow Eleanor to France, and his later discovery that his true father was Richard I, are all cut. In place of Shakespeare's increasingly fragmented presentation of complex action spread over almost a dozen different locations, Cibber offers a neat division between three acts set in France and a final two in England. Even he, however, was obliged to employ a number of different settings in the last act: the walls of a castle, a room of state, a field, and the neighbourhood of Swinstead Abbey. Act V begins with Arthur's death-leap from the walls of the castle (IV.iii in Shakespeare's text), after which he is 'covered by a parapet between his body and the audience'. Hubert and assorted lords discover the body, and Salisbury, refusing, unlike his Shakespearean counterpart, to believe Hubert's protestations of innocence, stabs and kills him. In the final sequence of action Arthur's funeral procession is seen moving towards the Abbey with Constance in attendance. (Unlike Shakespeare's character, this Constance is still alive at the end of the play.) John, again in contrast to the Shakespearean character, asks Heaven for mercy, and word is brought that Blanche has arrived and persuaded the Dauphin to lay down his arms. In place of Shakespeare's final words – 'Naught shall make us rue / If England to itself do rest but true!' – Cibber concludes: '*England* no foreign force shall e'er subdue / While prince and subject to themselves are true!'

In the same year that *Papal Tyranny* and the Garrick revival of *King John* were performed, 'A letter to Colley Cibber, Esq; on his Transformation of *King John*' (unsigned, but, probably, Brian Vickers, the editor of *The Critical Heritage*, suggests, by the author of 'The Occasional Prompter' series in *The Daily Journal*, 1736–37) took Cibber to task for his avowed intention to make *King John* '*more a Play than what you found it in Shakespeare*' (p. 155). Of all Shakespeare's plays, the writer

[7]

considers this is the one 'which sins most against the three Grand Unities of the Stage, *Time*, *Place* and *Action*, and is on that Account the less reducible to *Rule*' (*ibid.*, pp. 155–6). In addition, though Cibber has 'purg'd *Shakespeare* of his *low Stuff*', he has simply 'fill'd the Place up with *Flat*' (*ibid.*, p. 157). His characterisations of Faulconbridge and Constance are weak and thin compared to Shakespeare's vibrantly realised creations, and, in the crucial scenes between John and Philip and John and Pandulph, where the '*inspiriting* Quality ought to have been, according to [Cibber's] Declaration, infused with a lavish Hand', the writer 'can find nothing of it. I observe indeed', he continues, 'you have considerably *lengthened* the Scene; spun out the Dialogue; made *John declaim, argue, confute, puzzle* the Cardinal himself with Doctrine: but what of all that? where is the *Inspiriting?*' (*ibid.*, p. 159). Cibber's rendering of the scene in which John persuades Hubert to agree to Arthur's death is so tamely done that 'if it was not for a few Lines here and there of *Shakespeare* retained we shou'd see the whole Scene without any *great Pain* or *Terror*' (*ibid.*, p. 160). *Papal Tyranny* will, the writer affirms, 'inspire future Amenders of [Shakespeare], and be as a Land-Mark to them to escape the Perils that wait upon such hardy bold Attempts!' (*ibid.*, p. 162).

It would be difficult certainly to defend Cibber in the face of the accusation that, having omitted all the bits of *King John* he considered unsuitable, he proceeded to fill 'the Place up with *Flat*'. Instead of Pandulph's casuistical dexterity and John's impassioned, if short-lived, outburst of defiant anger, he offers little but bombastic speeches in the course of which the two men alternately lambast each other to little real purpose. When Shakespeare's Pandulph, for example, enquires why John has refused to accept Stephen Langton, the papal appointee, as archbishop of Canterbury, John replies:

What earthy name to interrogatories
Can task the free breath of a sacred king?
Than canst not, Cardinal, devise a name
So slight, unworthy, and ridiculous,
To charge me to an answer, as the Pope.

Tell him this tale, and from the mouth of England
Add thus much more: that no Italian priest
Shall tithe or toll in our dominions;
But as we, under God, are supreme head,
So, under Him, that great supremacy
Where we do reign we will alone uphold,
Without th'assistance of a mortal hand.
So tell the Pope, all reverence set apart
To him and his usurped authority. (III.i.147–60)

Here, John's vehemence is directed against the Pope, the man whose hand he defines as merely mortal, not that of God's representative on earth, and whose authority is usurped, not divinely sanctioned. The placing of the word 'Cardinal' half way through the third line, preceded and followed by a slight pause, links it rhythmically with 'Pope', that 'slight, unworthy and ridiculous' name. Both men, John declares, are insignificant, their power merely a pretence. Cibber's equivalent speech is as follows:

I tell thee, legate, as to *Lancton's* right,
One pope's enough for *England* to endure!
But viceroys there we never will receive,
For such are all when *Rome* appoints our pastors!
Created from abroad, they know no lord at home;
But, when their duty's question'd, answer *Rome*!
Rome shall support them; for their king's her vassal!
But, cardinal, from hence imperious *Rome*
Shall know, in *England* we will reign!
Nor shall, while we have life, *Italian* priests
Have tithe or toil in our dominions!

(*Dramatic Works*, p. 168)

Setting aside the fact that Cibber's language is less forceful than Shakespeare's, the essential difference between the two speeches lies in the emphasis on the word 'Pope' in the former and 'Rome' in the latter. Shakespeare's John is aware of the danger Langton might pose, but his anger is directed mainly towards the Pope,

[9]

the mere mortal who dares to interfere in his affairs. King John in *Papal Tyranny*, on the other hand, is primarily concerned with the fact that the 'pastors' created by the Pope would owe their allegiance to a foreign power. It is not one 'Italian priest' that is at issue here, but priests in the plural. Protestant England must be saved from the insidious designs of Rome.

It was Cibber's intention, as it had been Bale's, and that of the author of *The Troublesome Reign*, to present a clear division between John as Protestant hero and Pandulph as the agent of a hostile Catholicism. To achieve this he had to clarify and simplify Shakespeare's more complex and sometimes ambiguous model. In order to strengthen the equation of a virtuous Protestantism with Englishness, for example, Cibber alters the motivation of the English lords who, in Shakespeare's *King John*, join forces with the Dauphin for reasons which can be seen as self-serving and unpatriotic. In *Papal Tyranny* their enmity against John is occasioned by a factor which receives no mention in Shakespeare's play, the desire that John will sign the charter, which will 'to ages hence / Record our ample rights and liberties'. Once this is achieved, their next concern will be 'to dismiss in peace the arms of *France*'. The lords are successful in their aims. In the last act, shortly before the dying John is brought on stage, Salisbury remarks: 'How fortunate the hour! that he had sense / To ratify our rights and seal the charter.'

In the final act of *Papal Tyranny*, in contrast to *King John*, Constance is present onstage and Blanche performs an important offstage function. Constance is an odd hybrid in this play, because, though she retains some of the impassioned lines of Shakespeare's character and, in fact, becomes the advocate of an Anglo-French attempt to destroy Angiers in place of the Bastard, who makes this suggestion in Shakespeare's play, her chief role, like that of Blanche, is as a representative of the 'feminine' virtues. When the Abbot repudiates her proposal as a 'resource of female spleen', she too rejects it: 'Rather let *Angiers* know a lawless lord / Than to the rightful be their lives a sacrifice.' Her exit lines in Act III, after her lamentations over her imprisoned son, present her as a gentle female animal who will die in a helpless attempt to protect her young.

> So when the fawn the hunter's toils have snar'd,
> The bounding doe forsakes the safer herd;
> Wild o'er the fields to his vain help she flies,
> And, pressed by fear, on pointed javelins dies. (p. 280)

In the event, she doesn't die, but survives to forgive John and thank God that her 'afflictions have subdued [her] soul' so that she can behave charitably even to her enemy.

While Constance's role as self-sacrificing mother is complicated by the anger which at times she has difficulty in suppressing, Blanche is an ideally submissive figure. Hearing of John's intended departure for England in Act II, she tells the French king that it

> Alarms my heart with fears till now unknown:
> When he's away, and I left here a stranger,
> Young, unexperienc'd, liable to failures,
> How may simplicity, tho' well inclin'd,
> Mistake the duties of a bride or daughter?
> Without his guidance to direct my steps,
> How may my errors wander from your favour? (p. 266)

Blanche's one positive action, her persuading of the Dauphin to end the war, occurs both offstage and in accordance with her womanly role as supplicant for others. As a character, she is merely a cipher, a pallid representative not of an individual person but of the acceptable face of young, docile womanhood.

Further adaptations
In 1800 the Rev. Richard Valpy adapted Shakespeare's play for performance by the boys of Reading Grammar School. Like Cibber, Valpy omitted the whole of the first act. Like his predecessor, he attempted to modernise and 'refine' Shakespeare's language, and in doing so destroyed the power of the original. Constance's lines: 'I will instruct my sorrows to be proud / For grief is proud and makes his owner stoop', for example, became in the Valpy version: 'I will instruct my sorrows to be proud /

For grief is proud and dignifies the mourner' (quoted by Odell in *Shakespeare from Betterton to Irving*, p. 71), with the effect that Shakespeare's skill in placing the homely and onomatopoeic 'stoop' as the final word in the thought process is entirely negated by the substitution of the grander, but far less resonant, 'dignifies' and by the choice of the soft-sounding 'mourner' as the concluding word.

On 20 May 1803 Valpy's *King John* received a further performance, this time at Covent Garden. The title-page of the printed text of the play reads: '*King John*, an Historical Tragedy (altered from Shakespeare), as it was acted at Reading School, for the Subscription to the Naval Pillar, to be Erected in Honor of the Naval Victories of the War; and as it is now performing at the Theatre-Royal, Covent Garden, with Distinguished Applause. Reading 1803' (*ibid.*, p. 70). Like *Papal Tyranny*, Valpy's *King John* received a performance at a major theatre because it capitalised on the current atmosphere of public danger. In the following year, in his revival of Shakespeare's *King John*, John Philip Kemble responded to the continuing Napoleonic threat with the insertion of the following lines at the end of V.i.

> Sweep off these base invaders from the land:
> And above all exterminate those slaves,
> Those British slaves, whose prostituted souls,
> Under French banners, move in vile rebellion,
> Against their king, their country, and their God.

Kemble's acting version of *King John* substantially reduced the number of lines, as did others of the period. In *William Charles Macready's King John*, Charles H. Shattuck's comparison of acting versions reveals that Garrick's consisted of approximately 1,905 lines, John Philip Kemble's about 1,690 lines and Macready's 1,830 lines, as against 2,570 in the original (p. 10). Frequently, lines were cut either to strengthen the focus on John and his claim to the English throne or because they were perceived as indelicate. Scenes which involved French characters were considerably reduced in length, as were references to the English lords' alliance with the Dauphin. Eleanor's allusions to the shaky basis of John's right to be king, notably his 'unsured assurance to the crown' (II.i.471), disappeared. In the 1770s the critic Francis Gentleman had expressed the view that the Bastard's 'blunt, sportive method of expression, tainted too with licentiousness, is abominable stuff', and his language at the end of Act I 'more suitable to the bully of a brothel, than a person of good sense, good breeding and real spirit' (quoted by Sprague in *Shakespeare's Histories*, pp. 13–14). Gentleman advocated the omission of Act I in its entirety, and though, as editor of Bell's Shakespeare, he did not himself follow this course of action, Valpy's subsequent understanding of the susceptibilities of his audience is shown by the fact that, when John Philip Kemble restored Act I in 1804, *The Monthly Mirror* protested that it should be 'totally expunged' as it contained 'indecencies which render it almost infamous for a modest family to be present at the performance' (*ibid.*, p. 14). In the light of these continuing depredations on Shakespeare's text, therefore, it would seem that a poem of 1750 entitled 'Shakespeare's Ghost' was of only limited effectiveness. The poem is addressed to the contemporary Shakespearean actor who is asked to rescue Shakespeare's words from the hands of his adaptors.

> To thee, my great restorer, must belong
> The task to vindicate my injur'd song,
> To place each character in proper light,
> To speak my words and do my meaning right,
> To save me from a dire impending fate,
> Nor yield me up to Cibber and to Tate:
> Retrieve the scenes already snatched away,
> Yet, take them back, nor let me fall their prey:
> My genuine thoughts when by thy voice exprest,
> Shall still be deemed the greatest and the best.
>
> (quoted in *The Critical Heritage*, p. 382)

Though they may not have restored all Shakespeare's words, however, eighteenth- and nineteenth-century actors established a degree of popularity for *King John* unequalled before or since. The final couplet, therefore, is a valid representation of the actor/author relationship at the time: 'So by each other's aid we both shall live / I fame to thee, thou life to me shalt give.'

Popularity in the eighteenth and nineteenth centuries

For a little over a hundred years following the 1745 revival *King John* was frequently performed on the London stage and, to a slightly lesser degree, in the provinces and in North America. Its popularity during this period is attributable partly to the early nineteenth-century fascination with historical accuracy in the staging of Shakespeare's plays (discussed in Chapter II), and partly to actors' and audiences' enjoyment of the high emotional moments of the play. Major actors and actresses of the day 'vied with each other in the principal roles' (Waith, '*King John* and the drama of history', p. 193). Garrick, John Philip Kemble, Macready, Samuel Phelps and Charles Kean all played John, and Phelps and Macready also played Hubert. Charles Kemble played the Bastard, as also did Garrick. Mrs Cibber, Sarah Siddons and Helen Faucit were notable Constances. In contrast to twentieth-century critical opinion, which has focused largely on *King John*'s apparent lack of thematic and dramatic coherence, eighteenth- and nineteenth-century critics and audiences paid a good deal of attention to key roles and scenes. Mrs Inchbald, writing in 1808, expressed the view that Constance, not John, was 'the favourite part both of the poet and the audience' (*Shakespeare's Histories*, p. 20). Thomas Davies, in the 1780s, was particularly impressed by the scenes of pity and terror in the third act. Act III, scene iii, the 'interview between John and Hubert, where the king solicits Hubert, more by looks and actions than by words, to murder his nephew Arthur' was, he believed, 'in the opinion of every man of taste, superior to all praise' (quoted in Scott and Williamson, *Shakespearean Criticism*, p. 217).

The second Hubert/John scene (in IV.ii), the Hubert/Arthur scene, John's death scene and Constance's speeches in III.i. and III.iv. were also highly acclaimed. The tendency of critics and audiences during this period to concentrate on favourite characters and scenes and to respond to the play as a sequence of dramatic moments rather than to search for overall coherence was, Waith suggests, particularly suited to the 'notoriously episodic' nature of *King John* (p. 199). Theatregoers of the time were used to evaluating different actors' portrayals of key scenes and speeches in a similar way to that in which an 'opera critic would naturally compare, say, Nilson's Liebestod with Flagstad's' (*ibid.*, p. 198). Two of the greatest interpreters of King John were Kemble and Macready. Though a number of critics found Kemble's John 'too artificial and too cold', Boaden, in his *Memoirs of the Life of John Philip Kemble Esq.*, attested to the power of the 'noiseless horror' in his portrayal of the 'great scene with Hubert' (*ibid.*, p. 195). In *Shakespeare and the Actors*, Sprague describes Macready's version of this scene:

> Macready, after uttering the word 'death,' 'started back appalled by the sense of having overleaped all safety'; then gazed 'in terror on the witness to the sound . . . in agony of suspense to know how he received it.' Like Kemble he had glanced first at the young prince, and made this glance an 'index to the dark deed.' But 'when he pronounces the word "death!" he does not look in Hubert's face.' Frith reports that when this John threw off the mask 'and in two words, *"the grave,"* ' made his meaning unmistakable, he 'placed his mouth close to Hubert's ear' and whispered them; yet the whisper 'could be heard at the back of Drury Lane gallery.' (p. 112)

Waith's analogy of an opera critic's characteristic response is particularly apposite to Constance's intricate, rhetorical expressions of grief. According to Thomas Davies, Mrs Cibber delivered the words, 'O Lord! my boy' in her final speech 'with such an emphatical scream of agony as will never be forgotten by those who heard her' (Waith, p. 194). Sarah Siddons, who succeeded Mrs Cibber in the role, was, in the view of most of her contemporaries, an unsurpassable Constance, both in the power of her performance and in her expression of the character's feelings for her son. For her biographer, Thomas Campbell, 'she became "the embodied image of maternal love and intrepidity"' (*ibid.*, p. 198). George Fletcher was of the opinion, however, that Sarah Siddons concentrated too much on Constance's '"ambition", made her too tigerlike', whereas Helen Faucit portrayed the 'tenderness and the poetry of . . . maternal affection', and revealed the 'essentially feminine' nature of the character (Shattuck, pp. 50 and 51). Faucit's

Constance and Macready's John are discussed in more detail in the following chapter.

Both Campbell and Fletcher stressed Constance's maternal qualities. In an essay of 1833, Anna Brownell Jameson also emphasised this aspect of Constance: 'Whenever we think of Constance, it is in her maternal character', she wrote. She noted, too, Constance's credibility as a human being. 'The action calls forth her maternal feelings, and places them in the most prominent point of view; but with Constance, as with a real human being, the maternal affections are a powerful instinct, modified by other faculties, sentiments, and impulses, making up the individual character' (quoted in *Shakespearean Criticism*, p. 220). Later in the nineteenth century, however, critical opinion found Constance unconvincing. Hudson, writing in 1872, had little sympathy for her use of rhetoric, which he considered to be frequently redundant, and 'at the turn of the century' a number of critics 'found her guilty of rant' (*Shakespeare's Histories*, p. 22). When Julia Neilson played the role in 1899, a reviewer dismissed Constance's 'hysterical grief' as 'overdone'. Mrs Siddons had, he commented, reputedly shed 'real tears', but that was, after all, 'in the sentimental age . . . I sometimes think', he continued, 'Mrs. Siddons must have been what the Americans call "a holy terror"' (Waith, p. 200).

Critical sympathy for John also waned in the later years of the nineteenth century. Edward Dowden, for example, castigated him as 'wretched and cowardly' and Fredrick Boas was of the opinion that he was '"the least consistent" of all Shakespeare's kings' (*Shakespearean Criticism*, p. 206). The Bastard, by contrast, has increasingly gained in popularity, becoming, in the twentieth century, the one constituent element of the play that has met with almost universal approval.

Twentieth-century responses

Though it has had its supporters, *King John* has not been a popular play in the twentieth century. Prior to the First World War, a review of the Shakespeare Memorial Theatre production with F. R. Benson as John, in the *Stratford-upon-Avon Herald* (29 August 1913), observed that 'despite the beauty of many of its lines', *King John* could not 'be accepted as a very interesting or good acting play'. A little over thirty years later, according to Sprague, *King John* was 'almost unknown as an acting play' (*Shakespeare and the Actors*, 108). The fact that it is still little known or appreciated is evident from Lyn Gardner's enthusiastic response to the 1988 RSC production which led her to question 'why *King John* is generally dismissed as a stinker (and so seldom performed)' (*City Limits*, 2 June 1988).

Part of the explanation for *King John*'s demotion to the status of a 'stinker' lies in the already noted lessening of sympathy for John and Constance towards the end of the nineteenth century. Arthur, too, has suffered a similar fate. Whereas for William Hazlitt the scene in which the young prince pleads with his gaoler to spare his eyes was the most moving part of the play – 'If any thing ever was penned, heart- piercing, mixing the extremes of terror and pity, of that which shocks and that which soothes the mind, it is this scene' (*Shakespearean Criticism*, p. 219) – a review in the *The Sunday Times*, a hundred years later, found it 'affecting schoolboy stuff' (16 November 1924). In the 1930s, John Dover Wilson refuted Edmond Malone's citation of the importance of Shakespeare's son's death in determining the date of composition of *King John*:

> if the much-praised, and over-praised, portrait of the boy Arthur be really the dramatist's obituary notice of his own son, as many have supposed, his paternal affection must have been conventional and frigid to a degree which is very difficult to reconcile with the tender and passionate nature that gives warmth and reality to his later dramas. Indeed, if the death of Hamnet Shakespeare in 1596 meant anything to Shakespeare, Constance's lamentations must surely have been written before that event taught him what true grief was. (Cambridge ed., p. vii)

The more naturalistic performance style of the twentieth century has also created problems for actors in the roles of John, Constance and Arthur. They have been 'caught between a rock and a hard place, for they would be damned whether they played with the full expression that the lines invite or with muted understatement' (New Cambridge ed., p. 11). Constance's highly complex, rhetorical speeches of lamentation are particularly problematic because they invite expression in a heightened, declamatory style of performance which a modern susceptibility finds artificial and unconvincing. The contemporary practice of casting a boy as Arthur, instead of a young actress, as in the eighteenth and nineteenth centuries, has probably added to the difficulties of this role, as Arthur's formalised pleas for clemency in his scene with Hubert require a technical expertise beyond the reach of most twentieth-century boy actors.

A further problem presented by *King John* is that, with the single exception of *Henry VIII*, it is Shakespeare's only dramatisation of English history which does not belong within a related cycle of plays. The remaining history plays, the two tetralogies, deal with consecutive events in English history, from the deposition of one Richard to the defeat of another by the first Tudor monarch, and twentieth-century critics and theatre practitioners have increasingly viewed the sequence as a narrative and thematic whole. Intricate parallels and patternings connect the eight plays, so that a knowledge of one gives substance and focus to an understanding of each of the others, as vital questions pertaining to the use and abuse of power are examined over a period of nearly a hundred years. *King John*, by contrast, is a story 'told in a vacuum' (New Penguin ed., p. 8). It 'stands alone' and 'its finale is final' (Vaughan, 'Between tetralogies', p. 408). At the end of the play, as is the case in *Richard III*, a Henry is present who will become king of England, but, in place of the victorious soldier Henry Tudor, there is a hesitant young man who has not even been mentioned until this point in the play. Even the patriotic elements of *King John*, once so popular, have in recent times become suspect, as the radical reinterpretation of the Bastard in Deborah Warner's 1988/89 RSC production made clear. In addition, in place of an earlier response which situated the play's power and pathos in individual scenes and moments, twentieth-century scholarship has sought, and frequently failed to find, an overall political meaning. Attention has focused on the play's apparent lack of coherence: its episodic and fragmentary structure, the absence of a clear sense of ending, and the unsatisfactory nature of John himself as unifying agent.

The 'least dramatically magnetic of all Shakespeare's kings'
Twentieth-century accusations against the eponymous character of *King John* can be summarised as follows: John is intrinsically uninteresting, he behaves inconsistently, and he fails to unite the various disparate elements of the play. For Gareth Lloyd Evans, for example, he 'is the least dramatically magnetic of all Shakespeare's kings [who] almost slides his way through [the] play . . . it is as if King John is the only monarch of English history whom Shakespeare found not only uninteresting but incapable of striking fire from his imagination' (*Shakespeare II*, pp. 37 and 38). A review in *The Birmingham Post* (24 April 1925) of a production at the Stratford Memorial Theatre praised Randle Ayrton's performance as John because he 'was the wicked man whose wickedness is not so consistent as to become greatness, which is as Shakespeare represented the King'. In the opinion of the reviewer it was 'Faulconbridge, the bastard of Richard, and not the mean, treacherous, clever King John who [made] the play interesting'.

It is notoriously difficult to designate John as either hero or villain of the piece, his 'meanness' and 'treachery' disqualifying him from the former role, his equivocation over the murder of Arthur mitigating the force of his villainy. Above all, he lacks staying power and a clear sense of purpose. Though he acts with energy and decisiveness in the early scenes of the play, he later loses momentum, handing over authority to the Bastard and eventually dwindling, in his own words, to become 'a scribbled form, drawn with a pen / Upon a parchment' (V.vii.32–3) and now crumbling to ash. Even in the early section of the play, when John is still a forceful figure, he offers few clues as to what is going on in his mind, and, in the final scenes, his responses never seem adequate to the consequences of his own actions or the external pressure of events. He does, it is

true, say, 'I repent' with regard to Arthur's death, but not only
are these two words woefully inadequate as an expression of
remorse, they are also made in the context of the lords' anger
and his own consequent danger. His attempt, at the end of IV.ii,
to place the guilt of the murder on Hubert's shoulders, though
unedifying, appears at least to show some consciousness of the
gravity of the deed; but the moment he hears that Arthur is in
fact still alive the anguish and horror disappear:

> Doth Arthur live? O, haste thee to the peers!
> Throw this report on their incensèd rage
> And make them tame to their obedience.
>
> (IV.ii.260–2)

Neither hero nor villain, a man without consistency of purpose for good or ill, John is a difficult character to respond to
with either warmth or dislike. Perhaps, if the play lacks a
centre, this is because John himself lacks one. It is hard to know
what is going on in John's mind because he so rarely tells us. He
is alone on stage only once, and he then speaks his only soliloquy, which consists of three words: 'My mother dead!'
(IV.ii.181). As a possible indication of John's deep-seated reli-
ance on the forceful Eleanor, the words are revealing, but they
can serve only as a form of shorthand for a deeper expression of
John's psyche. Perhaps the closest an audience or reader can
get to a delineation of John's inner landscape is in III.iii, where,
verbally, he transforms the sunny daytime world into a graveyard in which 'melancholy' would bake the blood, and Hubert,
without the assistance of his bodily senses, would understand
and accede to John's purpose. His words here are horrifyingly
suggestive of a personal hell, but, prophetically, it is a hell
notable chiefly for its insubstantiality of form. If John is the
'least dramatically magnetic of all Shakespeare's kings', this is
largely because he is also the one most lacking in inner substance. In the English history plays, Shakespeare frequently
explores the relationship between the two roles of a king: the
body (and mental attributes) of the individual man, and the
ruler of the body politic. John's physical body, burnt up by a
corrosive poison, is emblematic of England, torn apart by war-

ring factions. John the man, however, resists definition. Even in death he offers us little insight into his inner self. His final words present his death solely in terms of his public function as king: 'all this thou seest is but a clod / And module of confounded royalty' (V.vii.57–8)

'A good enough railer'

A survey of twentieth-century reviews of *King John* highlights the difficulties facing an actress undertaking the role of Constance during the last hundred years, for, whether she invested the lines with all their inherent histrionic fervour or attempted a more naturalistic tone, her efforts were unlikely to meet with general approval. *The Birmingham Post* of 24 April 1925, for example, considered that 'Miss Florence Saunders as Queen Constance . . . evidently possessed a score which read pianissimo where we should read fortissimo, for she did not realise the character of Constance as manifested by ranting rhetoric and tumultuous action'. In 1957, *The Times*'s reviewer was still offering similar advice: 'Miss Joan Miller has the difficult part of Constance. She tries to speak her wild and whirling words of love and grief realistically, and skilful as is the attempt, we realize that they are words that cannot be spoken, but must be declaimed with a surge of passion which no realistic treatment can produce' (17 April). Even when the actress succeeded in playing the lines 'fortissimo', she was likely to find herself dismissed as 'a good enough railer' (*Sunday Times*, 16 November 1924) or 'a believably intolerable Constance' (*The Times*, 21 March 1974).

Two recent articles, however, the first by Phyllis Rackin, the second by Juliet Dusinberre, offer new ways of viewing Constance and the other female characters in the play. Rackin argues that women in *King John* 'play more important and more varied roles than in any of Shakespeare's other English histories' and that, 'Like the ambiguous ethos of the play itself, the female characters . . . are deeply divided' ('Anti-historians', p. 338). Eleanor and Constance both champion their sons in the battle over the crown, but their traditional gender role as mothers, far from uniting them, has the opposite effect. The play's other mother, Lady Faulconbridge, as the only person who knows the truth about her son's paternity, points to the possibility that an 'adulterous woman . . . can make a mockery' of the notion of patrilineal succession (*ibid.*, p. 337). Blanche, 'cast in the familiar female role of a medium of exchange between men', becomes not the means of uniting the 'warring factions' but, instead, 'the embodiment of their divisions' (*ibid.*, p. 339). In Rackin's view, women characters are fundamentally unsettling in *King John* because they 'no longer serve their traditional functions as creators of male bonds and validators of male identity' (*ibid.*, p. 338). Juliet Dusinberre writes that Constance in her lines describing 'the state of [her] great grief . . . becomes . . . the locus for the conflict of power and powerlessness which shapes the whole play' ('*King John* and embarrassing women', p. 38). Of Lady Faulconbridge, she observes that her 'language of honesty' when she admits her liaison with Richard I 'liberates warmth and love into the frigid world of this play' (*ibid.*, p. 46). In Dusinberre's view: 'What is clear from reading the play – and Deborah Warner's 1988 production reinforced this impression – is that up till the end of Act 3 the dramatic action is dominated by the women characters' (*ibid.*, p. 40). For Dusinberre 'the play goes to pieces once the women leave the stage' (*ibid.*, p. 51). Though Dusinberre and Rackin offer somewhat different views of the precise structural role women characters play in *King John*, the former seeing them as a unifying element, the later as representative of the essentially divided nature of the play itself, both place the women very much in the centre of the play's events. From Rackin's perspective, the women characters, and especially Blanche, become emblematic of the fractures and opposed loyalties which constitute the play; from Dusinberre's, Constance is the centre which can no longer hold once she is banished from the action.

A search for coherence
The fundamental criticism which has been levelled against *King John* in the twentieth century is that it is poorly constructed.

Like Colley Cibber and his vain search in Shakespeare's play for a piece of theatre structured around the unities of time, place and action, twentieth-century critics have sought (and often failed to find) a coherence of perspective and unified political design. In addition to the problem that John himself presents as the central character, the play has been seen as broken-backed, moving from the lengthy, debate-like Act II to an increasingly rapid and often bewildering succession of events and locations. Dusinberre notes the end of Act III as the point at which the play begins to fall apart, and certainly there is a crucial shift of focus around this point. The end of Act III marks the disappearance of the women, though also of Philip, the French king, who presumably becomes expendable when Cardinal Pandulph, the play's most accomplished politician, enters the action and takes the reins of power from his hands. It is noteworthy, however, that Pandulph is not present in the final five scenes, though his role in bringing the war to an end is reported. As is frequently the case in the last two acts, the motivating factors are offstage and distant. Indeed, it is often difficult to know who, if anyone, is in control of events. The gear-change from the bustle and bluster of the first half of the play, where self-interest and its effect on its victims are at least firmly in the public eye, to the fragmented, less comprehensible, more internalised world of the second half occurs in IV.i, which is in a new, plaintive and minor key. The focus is now on a helpless victim, and the agonising choice facing his gaoler: the setting, a dungeon, a hidden and secret place. Hubert's decision to protect Arthur regardless of the danger to himself is one of the few certainties of the final two acts, where incidents are piled thickly on top of each other, and often the link between cause and effect is obscure. Inconsistencies are not explained (John, for example, calls for Arthur's death in III.iii, but at the beginning of the next act Hubert shows his prisoner a warrant from the king which specifies that the child's eyes should be put out); and there are important gaps in the narrative. When Arthur escapes from prison, he is disguised as a 'ship-boy', though why he chooses this particular costume is not explained. The audience never

[23]

really learns the reason for John's second coronation, or what justification he has for telling the Bastard that he has 'a way to win [the lords'] loves again' (IV.ii.168) *before* he learns from Hubert that Arthur is still alive. Above all, the news that John is on the point of death, 'poisoned by a monk', is given without preparation. The lack of explanation and the intense compression of historical events – so that, as E. A. J. Honigmann notes, in IV.ii, practically the entire span of events in John's reign is 'crammed into one scene and made to seem simultaneous' (Arden ed., p. xxxi) – are not necessarily problematic in themselves. In any effective production of the play they are unlikely to be noticed. The real difficulty lies in the fact that the audience is given little guidance as to the significance of what happens. The Bastard, who earlier in the play offers a perspective from which to interpret events, is now frequently as much at a loss as the audience or the other characters. There is a disturbing sense that no one is any longer in charge. John slips out of life, the moment of his passing unnoticed. We hear that Pandulph has arranged a peace, but we are not shown this. Despite the Bastard's final, rousing words, it is easy to feel cheated as an unknown figure is hastily produced from the wings to fill the glaringly vacant throne.

Despite the problems it presents, *King John* has, however, not been without its champions. In the middle of the twentieth century, Lily Bess Campbell focused on parallels between John's reign and Elizabeth's, and saw *King John*, like the other history plays, as a 'mirror of Elizabethan Policy'. E. M. W. Tillyard 'emphasised the theme of rebellion and the theme of the true king . . . The authors of both of these influential books looked for the political meaning the plays might have had for an Elizabethan audience, and, in general, presented them as plays of ideas' (Waith, p. 192). In her 1984 essay, Virginia Mason Vaughan found the ending unsatisfactory in that the resolution of 'the problem of succession . . . is imposed from above, not within' ('Between tetralogies', p. 419), but argued that, in the play as a whole, 'an alternation between inflated claims of legitimacy and actions which undercut those claims' creates a shaping pattern, as is the case in the two parts of *Henry IV* and in *Henry V* (*ibid.*, p. 415). In the later scenes of *King John*, 'Abandoned strategies come back to haunt characters when they least expect it' (*ibid.*, p. 418). John realises that Arthur is necessary to his security only to find that the boy is dead, and Pandulph, after manipulating the Dauphin into fighting against John, is unable to persuade him to put an end to the hostilities when they no longer serve the Church's purpose.

Though some critics have viewed the Bastard as primarily a commentator on the action, and been of the opinion that, in Honigmann's words, the chorus 'however likeable . . . cannot be the hero' (Arden ed., p. lxxi), others have been willing to grant him the central and heroic function in the play that John has been seen to lack. Unlike John, the Bastard confides in the audience. He is engaging, amusing, usually honourable, above all likeable, where John is rarely any of these things. He constitutes, too, perhaps the only possibility of a consistent moral centre within the play, his identification of self-interest as the key motive of human action coming as a relief in a world where truth and honour seem merely expedient. Admittedly, he asserts his own right to pursue 'Commodity, the bias of the world', but, in the event, he fails to follow this course of action and remains faithful to John despite the defection of the English lords and his own recognition, over the body of the dead prince, of Arthur's rightful claim to the throne (IV.iii.142–5). For James L. Calderwood, '*King John* represents a dramatic crucible in which Shakespeare explores and tests two antagonistic ethical principles, Commodity and Honour. The opposition between Commodity, or scheming self-interest, and Honour, loyalty in general but in its highest form loyalty to the good of England, comprises a basic theme to which almost every action and character of the play is vitally related' ('Commodity and honour', p. 85). Adrien Bonjour argues that 'Shakespeare attained a remarkably balanced structure by a dynamic representation of two closely connected characters [John and the Bastard] whose evolution curves are, in their very contrast, almost perfectly symmetrical' ('The road to Swinstead Abbey', p. 273). So, as

John disintegrates, the Bastard grows in moral stature, and this becomes the central governing principle of the play. Smallwood too locates a major structuring principle of the play in the relationship between John and the Bastard, the collapse of the former and the growth in moral worth of the latter establishing 'the pattern of the play's final movement' (New Penguin ed., p. 36). Such is the reader's or audience's sympathy with and admiration for the Bastard that they are lured into viewing him as John's potential successor (and Smallwood sees in V.vi.37–8 a suggestion that the Bastard too is tempted to see himself in this light); but, at the end of the play, the Bastard swears allegiance to Henry – thus offering, through the image of loyalty and integrity he has come to represent, a guarantee of probable future stability.

For some late twentieth-century critics the play's fragmented structure is inherently linked to its characteristic presentation of events. Douglas C. Wixson analyses the dialectical nature of *King John*, which prevents an audience from sharing 'the view of any character for long', with the result that 'By refusing particular views Shakespeare encourages us to devise our own' ('Calm words folded up in smoke', p. 122). The frequent shifts of perception, therefore, lead to the creation of a kind of puzzle, the pieces of which the audience are invited to assemble. Phyllis Rackin's view of the female characters as embodiments of the divisions between the warring groups of men is linked to an interpretation of the play as revelatory of the fundamental instability of patriarchal power structures. Eugene M. Waith suggests that the general tendency of twentieth century Shakespearean scholarship, which has been 'to look first for a pattern of ideas', may have been misguided, in that it has obscured our appreciation of 'the power that critics once found in scene after scene' ('*King John* and the drama of history', p. 211). For eighteenth- and nineteenth-century audiences the play's appeal lay in the emotional intensity of key scenes, and in the actors' depiction of the major figures – a focus, in other words, 'on character rather than theme' (*ibid.*, p. 201). A search for thematic coherence may well have inhibited their twentieth-century counterparts from responding to Constance's 'gorgeous affliction' and being '"parched with a scorching fever" at King John's death' (*ibid.*, p. 211).

CHAPTER II

King John in the
nineteenth century

The Kemble/Planché *King John*

Though never a major favourite among Shakespeare's plays,
King John was generally popular with actors and audiences
from the 1800s to the 1870s. For the former it offered opportunities for impressive displays of emotion in a range of
virtuoso roles, for the latter vicarious moments of passionate
intensity and pathos. In addition, *King John*, with the many
possibilities it offorded for the spectacular recreation of a
romantic bygone age, played an important role in the establish-
ment of an 'archeological' (historically accurate) approach to
theatrical costume. Charles Kemble's November 1823 revival of
King John is a major milestone in this style of theatre.

According to the memoirs of the dramatist and antiquary
James Robinson Planché, the impetus for the complex programme of historical research, as a result of which 'a complete
reformation of dramatic costume' was to become 'inevitable
upon the English stage', came from a casual conversation between himself and Charles Kemble (Planché, *Recollections and
Reflections*, pp. 38–9). Kemble was in the process of planning a
revival of *King John* with Young in the title role and himself as
the Bastard, and when Planché complained to him that 'a
thousand pounds were frequently lavished on a Christmas

pantomime or an Easter spectacle, while the plays of Shake-speare were put upon the stage with make-shift scenery and, at the best, a new dress or two for the principal characters' (*ibid.*, pp. 35–6), Kemble invited him to undertake the necessary re-search and superintend the production. As Planché himself had little knowledge of costume at this time, he solicited the help of Samuel Meyrick, whose recently published *A Critical Inquiry into Ancient Arms and Armour* proved a valuable source of information, and another antiquary, Francis Douce, who loaned him his collection of illustrated manuscripts and a copy of Strutt's *Dress and Habits of the People of England*, with illustrations specially prepared for Douce by the author. In addition, Planché examined existing seals, shields, stained-glass windows and monuments from the time of *King John*. The eventual Act I costume for John was based on his effigy in the choir of Worcester Cathedral. The image from his Great Seal provided the inspiration for his battle-dress, while Faulcon-bridge at this point in the play was costumed in the style of a thirteenth-century knight in Malvern church. Every character, large or small, was dressed with the same meticulous attention to historical detail – a fact which did not find favour with all the members of the cast. In *Recollections and Reflections* Planché vividly conjures up these responses, plus the attitude of the first-night audience:

> Never shall I forget the dismay of some of the performers when they looked upon the flat-topped *chapeaux de fer* (*fer blanc*, I confess) of the twelfth century, which they irreverently stigmatized as *stewpans*! Nothing but the fact that the classical features of a Kemble were to be surmounted by a precisely similar abomination would, I think, have induced one of the rebellious barons to have appeared in it. They had no faith in me, and sulkily assumed their new and strange habiliments, in the full belief that they should be roared at by the audience. They *were* roared at; but in a much more agreeable way than they had contemplated. When the curtain rose, and discovered *King John* dressed as his effigy appears in Worcester Cathedral, surrounded by his barons sheathed in mail, with cylin-drical helmets and correct armorial shields, and his courtiers in the long tunics and mantles of the thirteenth century, there was a roar

of approbation, accompanied by four distinct rounds of applause, so general and so hearty, that the actors were astonished. (p. 38)

The Kemble/Planché *King John* was not the first occasion on which a greater historical accuracy, at least with regard to the costuming of the major roles, had been attempted on the English stage, but it was the first time that the past had been recreated on this kind of scale. In the 1770s, for example, Macklin had played the first act of *Macbeth* in a Scottish costume, but Lady Macbeth had worn a fashionable eighteenth-century gown throughout the performance. In a review of the 1823 *King John*, *Bell's Weekly Messenger* praised John Philip Kemble (Charles Kemble's brother) for the abolition of 'the *full-bottomed wig*, the *long waistcoats* and *square-toed shoes* in *Richard*, *Hamlet*, *Macbeth* and *Othello*', but added that the 'new and appropriate' costumes for Charles Kemble's revival had 'seldom been equalled for splendour and effect'. The reviewer looked forward with enthusiasm to the revival of all Shakespeare's history plays 'with the aid of costume appropriate to the period of the supposed action of the play' (30 November 1823: Odell, *Shakespeare*, p. 172).

The *Bell's Weekly Messenger* account stresses chiefly three attributes of the costumes: their splendour, their novelty and their appropriateness, an appropriateness defined by their historical veracity. What is seen as important, therefore, is not simply the spectacular nature of the costumes but, in addition, an approach to history which views the past as both distinct from the present (and therefore capturable through stage pictures which stress its picturesque differentness from the present day) and, at the same time, inherently linked with the present. From this latter perspective, the characters on the stage are seen as 'real' people, as is evidenced by the careful and realistic accuracy of their dress. By extension, the play's events gain an added authenticity and solidity that more intimately links the early thirteenth- and nineteenth-century worlds. A passage from Planché's *Recollections and Reflections* interestingly both reveals his own attitude to the relationship between the text in performance and those past events which form the play's subject matter, and raises important questions regarding the function of theatrical costume. Planché takes issue with the opinion recently expressed by a Mr Percy Fitzgerald that: '"There are certain conventional types of costume and illustration to which an audience is accustomed, and which indicate *sufficiently* the era to which the piece belongs; and this is all that is required – all that will harmonize with the grand objects of interest, the progress of character, and the action of the drama" – I am at a loss', he continues

> to conceive what he would consider a conventional type of costume to which an audience of the present day would feel accustomed – say, in the play just spoken of, *King John*.
>
> What *conventional* costume would he suggest for the historical characters of the Kings of England and France, the Duke of Austria, the Earls of Salisbury and Pembroke, and Queen Eleanor? He will be pleased to learn that Mrs. Siddons was of his opinion, and expressed herself to her brother Charles in precisely the same terms: 'It was sufficient for the dresses to be conventional.' I must regret that I had no conversation with her on the subject, for I should have much liked to have heard from her own lips her definition of the word 'conventional' as applied to costume or scenery. I can perfectly understand *King John* or any other historical play being acted in plain evening dress without any scenery at all, and interpreted by great actors interesting the audience to such a degree that imagination would supply the picturesque accessories to them as sufficiently as it does to the reader of the play in his study. But go one step beyond this: what conventional attire could be assumed by the performers that would be endured in these days by the least critical playgoers? If the king is to be crowned, what would be the conventional shape of the diadem? If a knight is to be armed, what would be the conventional character of the armour? (pp. 39– 40)

Planché here separates out an approach to performance which concentrates (as does the reader in his study) on the play's language, and offers visually a near neutrality which encourages individual members of the audience to imaginatively assemble the pictorial elements of the play-world, from one in which vital decisions regarding visual representation have already been taken on the audience's behalf. In addition, his querying of the value of a 'conventional' approach to costume has important ramifications, for, once it is decided to place an *actual* crown on the king's head, the question of what constitutes an 'appropriate' crown – and therefore implicitly also the question of a particular society's understanding of the nature of kingship – is raised. The complexities hinted at by Planché's dismissal of the value of convention were still, however, in the future. For the time being 'appropriateness' meant faithfulness to the period in which the play was set. The past was a knowable continuum which gave validity and meaning to the present. The notion that interpretations of the past are multiple and determined by the perspective of the viewer was a problem which lay in wait for the twentieth century. Macready's 1842 *King John* and later revivals by Charles Kean, Samuel Phelps, Beerbohm Tree and Robert Mantell were all significantly informed by a way of responding to the past which underwrote the Kemble/Planché *John*.

Macready's 1842 *King John*

We have had nothing so great as the revival of *King John*. We have had no celebration of English History and English Poetry, so worthy of a National Theatre . . . The rude heroic forms of the English past . . . are in this revival realized . . . The accoutrements are complete, from the helmet to the spur of each mailed warrior . . . The scenery has had the same attention. The council room, the field before and after battle, the fortifications of Angiers, the moated and embattled fortress of Northampton, the glitter of the Royal tent, the gloom of Swinstead Abbey; they have all the air of truth, the character of simple and strong fidelity. (*The Examiner*, 29 October 1842: Shattuck, *William Charles Macready's King John*, p. 1)

Though not all the reviews were as enthusiastic as this one, Macready's 1842 revival of *King John* at Drury Lane Theatre was a prestigious affair. The costume designs by Charles Hamilton Smith were based on Planché's earlier research. John's first costume, a rose-red gown 'with a flowered border', white belt, green jewelled gloves and golden robe with jewelled borders and collar, was again inspired by his effigy in Worcester Cathedral. Queen Eleanor's dress was taken from 'her effigy in the Abbey of Fontevrault' (Shattuck, p. 17). For the Faulconbridge family, however, Smith designed new and distinctive costumes. Planché had used 'some enamelled figures on King John's silver cup at King's Lynn' as the basis for Robert Faulconbridge's costume, which consisted of pink hose, grey coat and blue cloak. Smith designed 'a brown undergown and a white overgown with a huge blue lion rampant' and a yellow band 'falling across the chest from the right shoulder' (*ibid.*, p. 18). The Bastard wore a similar costume, and Lady Faulconbridge's gown had white squares, each likewise decorated with a blue lion surmounted by a yellow band – a costume decision which can surely have hardly aided Lady Faulconbridge's desire to keep her relationship with Richard Coeur-de-Lion a secret!

The creator of the scenic effects was William Telbin, at this stage still a young and relatively unknown artist but later a noted nineteenth-century scene painter. For Act I the setting was a large throne room with grey stone walls, hung with tapestries, and a ceiling composed of hammerbeam arches. On a dais, upstage centre, was placed John's blood-red throne beneath a similarly coloured canopy. Charles H. Shattuck, who provides a wealth of invaluable detail regarding the 1842 *John,* suggests that Telbin must have visited Angiers because the scene he prepared for Act II, though it treated 'the observed elements with poetic freedom', appeared, nevertheless, 'to have been derived from observations taken on the spot' (p. 24). The Hubert/ Arthur scene was set in an 'ominous vaulted chamber' in Northampton Castle, the walls of which were painted a gloomy olive grey. There were two practical doors, one, downstage left, hidden by a dark green tapestry, the other, in the back wall, locked with a key. A window stage right, in the embrasure of which there was a crucifix, was the apparent source of illumination in the room, though in fact this was an illusion created by paint on canvas, stage lights, lowered to enhance the gloomy atmosphere, being the actual means of lighting the scene. Downstage, right of centre, was a weighty antique- looking chair and table.

For the threatened blinding of Arthur, a '"pan of imitation fire," and a set of blinding irons painted "red hot"' were used (*ibid.*, p. 28). In the final scene, which depicted the orchard at Swinstead Abbey, 'Blue mediums' on a number of lights created the effect of moonlight. The dying John, who was brought in through a stage piece representing the gate of the abbey, was carried on a couch by six monks and accompanied by more than twenty other personages.

Throughout the performance the large stage of Drury Lane Theatre was constantly animated by the formation and reformation of large groups of additional characters. When John spoke the opening words of the play, Shattuck estimates that there were fifty-nine people on stage, and when the various armies and citizens of Angiers were all present in Act II, there were eighty-eight. A contemporary account of the production in *The Times* paid tribute to Macready's skill in creating 'an animated picture' through the use of large-scale dramatic movement, interspersed by moments of stillness: 'The grouping is admirably managed. The mailed figures now sink into stern tranquillity; now, when the martial fire touches them, they rouse from their lethargy and thirst for action' (*ibid.*, p. 11). Critics of the time also stressed the fact, however, that the magnificence of the visual elements of the performance was not simply gratuitous. The *Anthenaeum* observed: 'The best praise of this superb spectacle is, that it assists materially in carrying on the business of the play' (*ibid.*). For the *Spectator*, the entire performance was 'an embodied picture', composed of separate images, and yet constituting a whole, 'in a word, the scenes are a mute chorus, presenting in a visible shape those circumstances and comments which it was the office of the chorus to suggest to the audience when the scenic art was in its infancy' (*ibid.*, pp. 11–12). The spectacular historical reconstruction of the nineteenth century would appear, therefore, to have served a similar choric function to that which the Bastard has frequently been assigned in the twentieth. The magnificence of the costume and scenic design, the pageantry, the constantly evolving stage pictures, were, however, not the only focus of critical attention. The performances of the actors in key scenes were also the subject of extensive comment – and debate.

Key roles and performances
'The roles usually singled out for analysis – praise or blame' in the 1842 *King John* were, Shattuck notes, 'Macready's King John, Helen Faucit's Constance, James Anderson's Faulconbridge, Samuel Phelps's Hubert, and the Prince Arthur of the child actress, Miss Newcombe' (ibid., p. 46). Macready first played John in the 1822-23 season at Covent Garden, the season prior to that of the Planché/Kemble *King John*. He performed the role during a further six seasons (sometimes at Covent Garden, sometimes at Drury Lane) before the the 1842 revival. Over these twenty years, Macready's conception of John gradually crystallised. Whereas his predecessor, John Philip Kemble, had stressed above all the heroic and kingly qualities of the character, Macready emphasised his villainy and inconsistency, with the result that 'as Leigh Hunt would later declare, he was "more like the real historical King John, the vacillating, weak, wilful monarch, less poetical than petulant and a bully"' (*Dramatic Essays*, quoted in Shattuck, 47). In an essay in the *Monthly Repository* of February 1834, Charles Reese Pemberton praised Macready's new and intelligent reading of the role. 'You would have *seen him think*, and heard him speak his thoughts', he wrote (Shattuck, p. 47). In place of the customary 'swagger of independence [*sic*] and patriotism' shown by his predecessors in John's defiance of Pandulph (III.i.147–60), 'Macready threw into his manner and expression, the irritation of an aggrieved selfishness', demonstrative of the fact that his anger arose from papal 'encroachment on *his* privilege to tithe and tax' (*Shakespeare's Histories*, p. 16). Though other performances received a mixed response in 1842, Macready was generally praised, one critic finding John 'not only one of his finest conceptions, but almost perfect in execution', another describing his performance as 'the best which our modern stage is capable of producing'. Macready's interpretation of III.iii was a major source of interest, for he conceived this as the point in the

play at which John undergoes a crucial transformation, from the 'hero-king, yet incipiently vicious' of the first half to the 'coward-king and villain' of the later scenes (Shattuck, p. 48).

In order to highlight the 'dark transition' that took place in III.iii, Macready infused a high level of energy into the earlier scenes, to such a degree in fact that some critics complained that at times the noise was ear-splitting. Act III, scene ii, which is only ten lines in length, was extended through the addition of stage business. In Shakespeare's version the Bastard enters with the head of the archduke of Austria whom he has just killed in an offstage battle. After a four-line soliloquy, John enters with Arthur and Hubert, and a brief dialogue ensues between the Bastard and John. Speedily, the scene establishes the death of Austria, the capture of Arthur, and the possibility of victory if the English forces manage to build on their successes to date in the battle. In Macready's version, in front of a 'pair of flats, depicting a colorful landscape for a battlefield', representatives of the English and French armies fought each other from one side of the stage to another. The Bastard then entered from the left and Austria from the right, and a duel began, in the course of which they disappeared offstage right, still locked in mortal combat. When the triumphant Bastard returned, he carried with him not the head of Austria but his lion's skin, which he proceeded to hurl offstage. To the accompaniment of alarms and shouting, a number of the English lords entered from one side, while Arthur, John and his retinue entered from the other. John 'threw [Arthur] across the stage to Hubert', the remaining lines of dialogue were spoken and everyone exited to the noise of 'shouts' and 'charges'. As this gradually faded away, trumpet calls were heard 'answering each other – then a Retreat [was] sounded' (*ibid.*, p. 27).

Act III, scene iii. took place on another part of the battlefield: gloomy and forbidding this time, the colours of the landscape sombre, the sky stormy and grey. The sudden transition 'from political pageant' to 'dark tragedy' was further effected by 'melancholy and wailing' trumpet music and the slow entrance of groups of exhausted English soldiers. When Eleanor took the weeping Arthur aside, 'the battle-weary nobles all turned in upon each other, as if in conversation, so that "No face on the stage except Hubert's and John's [was] turned to the audience"' (*ibid.*, pp. 27–8). When John proposed Arthur's death, he looked away, unable to confront Hubert directly. It was, the *Spectator* claimed, 'a masterly exhibition of cowardly villainy'. For *The Examiner*, all trace of Plantagenet vanished from the character of John at this point, and 'like a lowering cloud, the change [hung] over the tragedy to the end' (*ibid.*, 49). In the death scene Macready emphasised the physical agony of the poisoned king. In 1834 Pemberton had described 'the face, now blazing, now ashy pale . . . the hard tension of the arms, as the hands gripped in life's last agony to the cushions of the couch, the stony death of the position in which the *body* sat for some seconds ere it fell back across the couch' (quoted in Sprague, *Shakespeare and the Actors*, p. 116). For the *Atlas* in 1842, however, the 'masculine and horrible' portrayal, though unquestionably powerful, went 'beyond the truth required by the poet and the public' (Shattuck, p. 49).

As Hubert, Samuel Phelps was also highly thought of by a considerable number of critics. The *Morning Post* (25 October 1842) contained this paragraph:

> As Hubert is the finest character in the poet's conception, so was it acted with the most consistent power . . . [Phelps] is one of the few living men who touch our hearts, and this, not by loud words and hurried delivery and strong tones (although his strength is plentiful), but by the the genial undercurrent of living feeling which is ever leaping and throbbing under the surface of his acting. He calls forth a tear by the only magic that can do so – the strong persuasion that his grief or passion is actually grappling with the very roots of his own heart. (quoted in Allen, *Samuel Phelps*, p. 59)

The *Literary Gazette* considered his performance second only to Macready's, and the *Spectator* praised 'His "rugged aspect, voice and manner, and the melting tenderness encased in that rough rind"' which so well fitted him for the role of Hubert. *John Bull*, though praising a number of aspects of his performance, was of the opinion, however, that Phelps concluded the blinding scene 'with more noise than was effective' (Shattuck, p. 52).

A number of critics also found Miss Newcombe's performance as Arthur over-loud, and, in addition, like Macready's portrayal of John's death, unnecessarily realistic. As Shattuck notes, 'The blinding scene, *John Bull* thought, was a mistake in taste, in which "reality is sought and poetry sacrificed." The child was "made to kick and scream, and in the turbulence of infantile terror to banish the sweetness and beauty of the poet."' *The Spectator*, though generally sympathetic to Miss Newcombe's performance, was of the opinion that in this scene she had been 'taught to give vent to her distress with the tearful dread of a child fearing bodily pain, rather than with that deeper-seated terror of the loss of sight which the language of the poet expresses'. By contrast, however, the *Examiner* considered that her 'downright energy gave new terrors and new beauties to the master-scene' (*ibid.*, p. 53). The *Athenaeum* objected to Arthur's death-leap in IV.iii, which it found ridiculously exaggerated. The actress jumped from a rostrum concealed behind a seemingly enormous tower, but actually, Shattuck estimates, approximately only twelve feet in height. Strategically placed in hiding were six men, waiting with a carpet to catch the prince, whom they then tumbled through the 'gateway down the steps onto the stage' (*ibid.*, p. 29) – a piece of stage business which would appear to be an interesting variation on the direction in Cibber's *Papal Tyranny* that 'Arthur leaps from the walls and is covered by a parapet between his body and the audience'. Sprague cites two further nineteenth-century solutions to the staging of this piece of action. In the first, Arthur jumped on to a bed and then crawled out, round the corner of a wall, and, in the second, the actress 'ran as if to take the leap, past a turreted part of the wall' and then slid down a perpendicular rod behind the turret, while a dummy was simultaneously thrown over the battlements, where it 'disappeared among the tangled grass beneath the wall'. The whole business was timed so that, 'as the "double" disappeared', the actress took up her position 'behind the "set piece" under the wall and raised [her] head to speak the last two lines' (*Shakespeare and the Actors*, p. 115). According to the Sadler's Wells prompt-book, Samuel Phelps employed an acrobat as a double 'who climbed out of a window and dropped down' (Shattuck, p. 29).

In 1842, two characters in particular were the source of adverse critical comment, both James Anderson as the Bastard and Helen Faucit as Constance being seen as inadequate by comparison with their illustrious predecessors, Charles Kemble and Sarah Siddons. For the majority of critics of the period Charles Kemble was, in the words of the *Spectator* critic, the only actor capable of expressing 'the physical grandeur and moral dignity of this noble specimen of valorous manhood' (Shattuck, p. 52). Accounts of Charles Kemble's portrayal stress his chivalrous and manly bearing, along with his easy elegance and wit. Mrs Cowden Clarke particularly admired 'his manly tenderness' with his mother (*Shakespeare and the Actors*, p. 109), while the painter W. P. Frith praised his 'elegant saunter' as he disappeared underneath the portcullis of Angiers, looking 'to the right and left with the insolence of a conqueror' (Planché, *Autobiography and Reminiscences* p. 21; Williamson, *Man of the Theatre*, pp. 132-3). Many critics thought James Anderson coarse by comparison and lacking in heroism. *John Bull* found his attitude to his mother 'devoid alike of respect and affection' and the *Spectator* pronounced him 'too much of the bully and swaggerer'. A dissenting view was offered, however, by the *Atlas,* which considered his performance 'masterly'. In the opinion of the *Atlas* critic, Anderson's 'caustic observation of men and manners' and 'the heroism of his grief over the body of his benefactor' were more effective, 'more true to Shakespeare than Charles Kemble's more smiling and polished effort' (Shattuck, p. 52). The critical response to James Anderson's Bastard is a pre-echo of opinions that would be voiced in the twentieth century concerning the portrayal of this character, particularly with regard to the consciously unheroic performance by David Morrissey in Deborah Warner's 1988/89 RSC production.

Though statuesque and beautiful, the twenty-five-year-old Helen Faucit was not physically strong, and her voice, though well suited to expressing tenderness, lacked sufficient power for the emotional tirades. Critical opinion in general applauded her 'earnestness' 'skill, and taste' but deplored her lack of ability to sustain the high emotional energy necessary for the role (*ibid.*, p. 50). In an essay he wrote for the *Athenaeum*, however, George Fletcher ardently supported Faucit's interpretation, which he found to be motivated by a depth of tenderness and a poetry of maternal affection missing from Siddons's over-ambitious and 'too tigerlike' portrayal. On the words: 'Here I and sorrows sit / Here is my throne. Bid kings come bow to it', at 'the climax of her grief', Helen Faucit looked up and raised 'her hand to play with the ringlets of her boy [who stood] stooping over her' (*ibid.*), with the effect, Fletcher writes, of at once deepening 'the impression of the preceding words and actions which make that sublime enthronement of her grief', and giving 'bolder effect to her majestically indignant contradiction of the French king's' following speech (Martin, *Helena Faucit*, p. 96). This Constance, in Fletcher's view, found the stimulus for her appeal to the heavens for aid against the 'perjured kings' in the embrace of her son. Rising to 'the natural height of her noble figure', she lifted her hands to heaven, and 'this exaltation of her figure' caused 'her piercing and scorching reproaches' of Austria's treachery to 'seem to be drawn down like the forked lightnings from above, searing and blasting where they strike'. Her appeal to Lewis's honour (III.i.316) was not played scornfully, in the manner of Mrs Siddons, but with nobility and 'generous fervour'. The excellence of Faucit's performance in Constance's final 'despairing scene', Fletcher writes, can be 'seen and heard, felt and wept over', but not adequately described. For his own part, however, he will long 'be haunted by those accents, now piercingly, now softly thrilling, now enamoured of death, now rushing back to the sweet and agonising remembrance of her child, now hurrying forward to anticipate the chasing of "the native beauty from his cheek," till her last lingering ray of hope expires, and reason totters on the verge of frenzy' (*ibid.*, pp. 96–8).

It is difficult at this distance in time to properly evaluate Fletcher's claims on behalf of Helen Faucit *vis-à-vis* Sarah

Siddons. Certainly, his comments on Siddons's lack of maternal tenderness would seem to be contradicted by the actress's own words with regard to her preparation for her entrance in III.i. In

> a famous passage she tells of how she was accustomed to stand, with Arthur beside her, listening to the march, as the French and English powers entered Angiers to ratify the marriage contract between Lewis and Lady Blanch: 'because the sickening sounds of that march would usually cause the bitter tears of rage, disappointment, betrayed confidence, baffled ambition, and, above all, the agonizing feelings of maternal affection to gush into my eyes.' (*Shakespeare's Histories*, p. 21)

Perhaps more problematic still, given the changes in performance style and the adoption of generally smaller, more intimate theatre venues, are the terms in which Siddons and Faucit were praised by their contemporaries. Siddons, herself, spoke of the 'gorgeous affliction' of Constance, and accounts of her acting in the role capture a sense of this quality in the actress, while Fletcher's descriptions of Helen Faucit are comparatively eulogistic. A twentieth-century sensibility can easily find these expressions embarrassingly effusive. The problem of course, with Constance, as a number of twentieth-century actress have discovered to their cost, is that it is a near impossibility to play her 'realistically'. All the characters in the play speak in verse. John's language is frequently histrionic; Arthur's appeals for clemency are highly stylised; and Pandulph's abstruse pronouncements are of a complexity that require enormous skill from an actor if an audience is to understand them at first hearing. No other character in the play, however, speaks a language which is both as rhetorical and yet as expressive of passion and despair as that of Constance. It could be argued that the large expanses of the Drury Lane and Covent Garden stages provided the most fitting setting for the expression of her grief.

Later nineteenth-century productions and Robert Mantell's *King John*

In August 1843 the Theatres Regulation Bill ended the monopoly previously held by Covent Garden and Drury Lane by granting all licensed theatres in London the right to perform plays. A few months later Samuel Phelps, who had played Hubert to Macready's John, became manager of Sadler's Wells with the intention of attempting to convert it into a 'legitimate' theatre. Sadler's Wells, as Shirley S. Allen explains 'had the longest history of any theatre in London, possibly in England'. The original wooden structure had been erected in the late seventeenth century by a Mr Sadler as a place of entertainment for the large numbers of people who were 'attracted to his garden by the discovery there of a buried medieval well to which miraculous healing powers were attributed' (*Samuel Phelps*, p. 77). The entertainment proved more popular than the holy well, however, and, in 1765, a stone theatre was built. At the beginning of the nineteenth century a large water tank was installed under the stage 'for the production of aquatic spectacles' and for thirty years Sadler's Wells became 'the home of the "nautical drama"' (*ibid.*, pp. 77–8). By 1840, the theatre offered its patrons a mixture of domestic pieces, farces, the occasional five-act play (despite the ban on performance by theatres other than the two patent house), and in addition such attractions as animal and tightrope acts. The excellence of the Sadler's Wells Christmas pantomimes was famed throughout London.

Phelps's first season at Sadler's Wells, which opened on 27 May 1844 with a production of *Macbeth*, was undeniably a risky venture. Though the stage dimensions were smaller than those of Covent Garden and Drury Lane, the pit was much larger, and Sadler's Wells could seat an audience of 2,600 in reasonable comfort, 'only a thousand less than the patent theatres' (*ibid.*, p. 79). The majority of the seats, however, were on pit benches (for a shilling) or sixpenny gallery seats. There were relatively few boxes, and it was here that wealthy patrons, who were also the chief supporters of Shakespearean drama, traditionally sat. It seemed unlikely that the less well off Sadler's Wells audience would prove as remunerative, or as enthusiastic about serious drama.

The size and enthusiasm of the first-night audience, therefore, took the management by surprise. 'Approximately twelve hundred persons thronged the gallery, and a thousand more crowded the benches in the pit. Even the boxes, at 2 shillings a seat, were filled to their capacity of six hundred' (*ibid.*, p. 84). Platforms had to be hastily erected so that those people who had not been lucky enough to get a seat would have some chance of seeing the stage. Though the actors occasionally found the reactions of the unsophisticated audience disconcerting, they repaid the rapt attention, interspersed with 'spontaneous cheers' or 'an awestruck shudder', with their 'best efforts' (*ibid.*, pp. 84–5). Unfortunately, few newspaper critics had attended the opening night, but, as *Macbeth* was succeeded by a repertoire which included *Othello*, *The Rivals*, *The School for Scandal*, *The Merchant of Venice* and Byron's *Werner*, an increasing number of accounts of the performances began to appear. In July *Hamlet* was performed for the first time, to enthusiastic reviews. The *Athenaeum* thought 'the gravedigger scene "almost magical in its effect"' (*ibid.*, p. 90), and a number of reviewers commented on the superb scenery and costumes. Phelps's Hamlet and the acting of the other members of the cast were generally commended.

At the end of September Phelps offered a production of *King John*, based on the Macready prompt-book, which brought audiences flocking from central London to the Islington theatre. Critical accounts compared the splendour and historical accuracy of the scenery and costumes with those of Macready's production. Of Phelps's John, 'one reviewer wrote: "He has more real genius in him than any actor of our time, and it is now making itself manifest . . . [his] personation of the monarch is extremely fine"' (*ibid.*, p. 90). Between the years 1844 and 1862 *King John* was performed at Sadler's Wells a total of sixty-five times. In November 1862 Phelps left Sadler's Wells, and, after a brief spell at the Lyceum, began an engagement at Drury Lane, where, in the 1865–67 season, he again played the role of King John.

Samuel Phelps's source for his copy of the 1842 prompt-book of *King John* was George Ellis, one of Macready's prompters. Ellis also later provided Charles Kean with a copy, plus 'water colors of Macready's scene designs' (Shattuck, p. 7). In 1846 Charles Kean staged *King John* at the Park Theatre in New York. The 'stage dimensions were very similar to those of Drury Lane' and Kean followed Macready's stage directions closely. He improved on the number of supernumeraries, however, with the result that one reviewer estimated that, in Act II, there were approximately two hundred people on the stage. The 'author of the humor sheet *Yankee Doodle*' ironically explained that 'THE SILENCE IN THE STREETS In the mornings now, is entirely owing to the performance of *King John* at the Park, – all the fish-men and ash-cart men having been engaged by Mr. Kean as trumpeters to "the borrowed Majesty of England"' (*ibid.*, p. 55). In February 1852, Kean produced *King John* at the Princess's Theatre in London, where *The Times* described it as 'one of the most complete representations known in the history of theatrical management' (*ibid.*, p. 57). In 1858 he revived *King John* as part of his farewell season. Shattuck writes that Kean was still following Macready's text and stage directions in his London productions. The Princess's Theatre was notably smaller than Drury Lane however, and, though some of the scenery was apparently derived from Telbin's original designs, other settings were new, Act I, for example, being 'copied from the Hall in Rochester Castle' (ibid.). Both in 1846 and 1852 a large engine of war formed part of the setting for Act II, with the result, in New York, that the scene change from the first to the second act sometimes took as long as fourteen minutes, as opposed to five under Macready at Drury Lane.

A late example of a production based on Macready's book of the play is afforded by Robert Mantell's *King John*, first performed at the Grand Opera House, Chicago, in 1907 and, in 1909, at the New Amsterdam Theatre in New York. Like Macready, Mantell emphasised John's lack of consistency, at one moment irascible, at another weakly irresolute. His treatment of the 'Temptation Scene' with Hubert 'was admirable for its investiture of wickedness with plausibility, and for its subtle transparency, – the suggestion of treachery, cruelty, and hideous crime being made in such a way that *Hubert's* acceptance of it and compliance with it seemed unconstrained and natural' (Winter, *Shakespeare on the Stage*, p. 511). Mantell's physical appearance, aided by stage make-up, intensified the effect of his performance. His eyes appeared cold and blue in his white face, his lips 'red, and sensual'. His hair, too, was red and a matted, red beard covered his cheeks. His movements were quick, sometimes 'spasmodic' and his 'trick of plucking at a single hair of the beard expressively denoted a nervous, splenetic temperament, overstrained and with difficulty held in check' (*ibid.*, pp. 512–13). The death scene, in the night-time orchard of Swinstead Abbey, was especially powerful. William Winter writes that around John were grouped courtiers and knights, some in full armour. His face was ghastly 'in the flickering light' and his voice in the final speeches 'gasping' and 'thread-like', so that it 'could be heard only with tears' (*ibid.*, p. 515).

In England, after the productions of the 1860s, *King John*'s popularity declined. A revival at Her Majesty's Theatre, London by Herbert Beerbohm Tree in 1899, however, provides a late – and extreme – example of the archaeological style initiated by Planché and Macready. Tree divided the play into three acts and added various tableaux, of which the most spectacular were the battle of Angiers and the granting of Magna Carta (neither of which events is shown in Shakespeare's play). He also introduced a good deal of stage business. Act I in the 'nobly vaulted chamber of Northampton Castle', opened with organ music and the majestic descent down a 'great staircase' of a 'portly chamberlain, wandbearing, red-robed', after whom skipped 'a little jester' (Beaurline, p. 19). In III.iii, in 'a glade of slim beeches' John whispered in Hubert's ear, while Eleanor watched 'with her eyes of ill omen'. Prince Arthur was picking daisies nearby, but, when the king smiled down at him in passing, Arthur started away. Some daisies were growing 'near the spot where the king ha[d] been whispering his behest.

Lightly, he [cut] the head off them with his sword' (Max Beerbohm, *More Theatres*, cited in Braunmuller, p. 87). In an account of the production in the *Saturday Review*, 30 September 1899, Max Beerbohm, Tree's half-brother, defended the additional pieces of stage business, on the grounds that they had brought vividly to life for him a play which in reading he had found 'insufferably tedious' (Waith, p. 206). On 21 September *The Times* also defended 'the interpolated tableau showing the granting of Magna Charta', observing that 'it completes the chronicle aspect of the play, and it supplies in itself a striking stage-picture' (Odell, p. 453).

The creation of striking stage-pictures was a vital part of all nineteenth-century productions of *King John*. 'Pictures', Waith writes, 'had a special fascination in [the] period of the early photographic experiments of Daguerre and Talbot. The word recurs frequently in dramatic criticism, whether or not it is a question of stage images.' Boaden had praised Kemble's skill in substituting 'his own face and figure for the *picture sense* of King John' and Kean 'credited Shakespeare with "impressing the imagination with living pictures of the Royal race"' (p. 208). An account of Macready's production in the *Illustrated London News* was especially enthusiastic about 'the last *tableau* of the tragedy', and considered that Macready's staging in general employed 'the glorious pageantry' to 'give true and beautiful aid to the living stream of poetry. Illustration makes beautifully perfect the grand illusions of the play' (29 October 1842: Waith, p. 207).

These comments are notably different in their emphasis from reviews of Beerbohm Tree's *King John*. For *The Times* reviewer, 'the history and the rhetoric' which had fascinated Elizabethan audiences verged on the tiresome, so that a picturesque setting became necessary 'as a gilding to the pill', while the *Athenaeum* remarked: 'a play such as *King John* is to be regarded as a vehicle for stage pageant' (Braunmuller, p. 86). Macready's visual recreation of a medieval world had been interpreted as an illustrative chorus which embodied the play's meaning. In place of Macready's connected stage pictures

[46]

which arguably informed and clarified audience response to the play, Tree would appear to have offered a sequence of images, spectacular in themselves but essentially discrete and separable. In light of Waith's reference to the importance of earlier 'photographic experiments', the seemingly filmic quality of Tree's pictures, each "frame" capable of being awarded a caption to delineate its desired effect, is worth noting. It is fascinating to learn, therefore, that Tree's inserted sequence of action showing the granting of Magna Carta was filmed, on London Embankment, and became, in fact, the first ever Shakespearean film – albeit of an event that does not occur in the original play (see Manvell, *Shakespeare and the Film*, p. 17).

CHAPTER III

Mid-twentieth-century productions

The popularity of *King John*, evidently waning in the latter years of the nineteenth century, continued to decline in the twentieth century. In the years between the First and Second World Wars there were productions at the Old Vic Theatre, in London, in 1921, 1926 and 1931, and at the Shakespeare Memorial Theatre, Stratford-upon-Avon, in 1925. Then, in 1940, after a fifteen-year gap, the Memorial Theatre mounted a new production. The following year *King John* was the opening play of the first Old Vic war-time season at the New Theatre, London. According to *The Times* review of the Shakespeare Memorial Theatre production, the reason for *King John*'s infrequent performance was that 'mere readers, as distinct from theatregoers' had 'pegged' its reputation at 'an unfairly low level' (9 May 1940). A play that on the page appeared to have few likeable characters, and was dull into the bargain, was surprisingly alive on the stage. W. H. Bush in the *Birmingham Gazette* was even more enthusiastic, finding 'Shakespeare's only play without a hero' also one of his 'most interesting plays' (8 May 1940). Unquestionably, however, the fact that *King John* can be interpreted as a play about patriotism added greatly to its popularity in the early years of the war. The timeliness of the *Birmingham Evening Despatch*'s comment that the play's final lines about an unconquered England 'must find an answer today in the heart of every Englishman' (8 May 1940), and of *The Times*'s reference to the Bastard 'standing so truculently and so humorously for the English spirit against whoever seems to threaten its survival' is vividly demonstrated by the following statement from the Memorial Theatre programme of the production:

Advice to audience
1. If the Air Raid Warning is given you will be told from the stage.
2. Remain seated. You are safer here than in the streets.
3. The performance will continue.
4. If anyone wants to leave the Theatre they will be shown out by the attendants.
5. Keep calm! Don't worry! The raiders may not be coming here!

The war intruded even into the reviews themselves. In the middle of *The Birmingham Post* review of 9 May 1940, immediately after the words 'The Bastard was the early champion of English unity', was printed: 'Black-out 9.16 p.m. to 4.51 a.m.'.

Nevertheless, when the 1948 Festival at the Shakespeare Memorial Theatre opened with a performance of *King John*, the memories of many of the reviewers appeared to be short-lived. The *Leamington Spa Courier* of 16 April considered the play 'not, perhaps, worthy of the occasion', and continued, 'It is a long time since *King John* was last produced at Stratford: it may well be as many years before it again appears in the repertory. It is a depressing work, and the general tenor of it hardly seems to justify the final affirmation as to England's greatness and security.' In general, reviews were more laudatory of the production than the play, though the *Daily Worker* of 16 April found *King John* 'one of Shakespeare's most strictly political plays – a far more realistic picture of a feudal carve-up than is found in most school textbooks', and the *Wolverhampton Express and Star* of the same day expressed the view that 'Of all the plays in the canon, *King John* is probably the most topical, for now, as then, national pledges and sacred oaths are cast aside to suit expediency'.

Michael Benthall's direction, in 1948, and Audrey Cruddas's set design were both reflective of the view that *King John* depicts 'the decay of England's greatness under the tyrant John' (programme note). Virtually all the reviewers praised the effectiveness of the staging: the beautifully sculpted groupings, the ebb and flow between motion and stillness. As the play's action became darker and more fractured, the single setting was gradually dismantled until at the end 'cracked walls and tattered standards' symbolised 'the rotten state of England' (*Coventry Standard*, 17 April). The stylisation of the setting was mirrored in a number of the performances. Drawing on a facility for expressive, compelling movement derived from his ballet training, Robert Helpmann portrayed a stealthy, decadent John, likened by Eric Keown in *Punch* to an emaciated King of Diamonds, while Paul Scofield was a foppish, 'delicately acidulous' King of France (*Coventry Evening Telegraph*, 16 April). Against the puppet-like artificiality of the kings, and the 'tittering, painted English court and grotesque citizens of Angiers' (*Birmingham Evening Despatch*, 16 April), Timothy Harley was an unaffected and poignant Arthur, and Anthony Quayle a life-like, down-to-earth Faulconbridge.

This was in contrast to the 1940 Memorial Theatre production by Iden Payne and Andrew Leigh, which had 'evolved the action in a series of handsome pictures bright with medieval blazonary' (*The Birmingham Post*). This production used scenery, in a manner more reminiscent of the nineteenth century, and George Skillan, as King John, 'by a coincidence of make-up [looked] very much like Sir Herbert Tree' (*ibid.*). The 1941 Old Vic production, like the 1948 Stratford *King John*, utilised a stylised setting. After the bombing of the Old Vic theatre in London in 1940, the company were evacuated to Burnley, and began a series of regional tours under the auspices of CEMA (the Committee for the Encouragement of Music and the Arts). *King John* opened at Lancaster Town Hall and played a variety of venues in the north of England and in Scotland before going to London. Partly, presumably, in response to the requirements of touring, the director, Tyrone Guthrie, staged the action against 'heraldic curtains' – 'sweeping banners' and 'bouncing hobby-horses before the walls of Angiers' adding to the non-naturalistic effect (Trewin, *Shakespeare on the English Stage*, p. 188). Ernest Milton, 'pallid, subtle, marsh-lit, in a stylised red wig' (*ibid.*) was an impressive John.

Two productions of the 1950s – the 1953 Old Vic *King John*, directed by George Devine, and Douglas Seale's 1957 production for the Shakespeare Memorial Theatre – afford an interesting contrast with regard to the kind of stylisation they employed in design and staging. This aspect of the two productions together with actors' interpretations of key roles and reviewers' responses to *King John*'s apparent lack of coherence, is considered in the following section.

The 1953 Old Vic production and the 1957 Stratford Memorial Theatre production

In 1953, three years after the reopening of the theatre, a five-year project to mount all the plays in the First Folio was initiated at the Old Vic. It was not the first time that the Old Vic had presented all thirty-six plays (this had previously been achieved between 1914 and 1923 – for the first time, according to Roger Wood and Mary Clarke, by any theatre), but the five-year programme which commenced in 1953 was conceived from the start as a systematic whole. The intention was to present, in repertory, one tragedy and one or two comedies each season, plus one or more of the history plays in chronological order. The 'Greek and Roman plays and the late plays of reconciliation would be fitted in where most appropriate' (Wood and Clarke, *Shakespeare at the Old Vic*, p. xiii). Prospective audiences would, therefore, have the opportunity of seeing all Shakespeare's plays in an interestingly varied, yet coherent, programme, within a relatively short space of time. Backstage space was very limited at the Old Vic and there was room for scenery only for the current production, and not for storage of other sets. In order to get round this difficulty, a permanent setting was created for all the plays in the 1953–54 season: *Hamlet*, *All's Well that Ends Well*, *King John*, *Twelfth Night*, *Coriolanus* and *The Tempest*. Designed by James Bailey, it consisted of three Palladian-style pillars a couple of feet behind the proscenium opening, and, upstage centre, a variety of stairways and levels, depending on the differing needs of the plays. In front of the proscenium was a forestage, which could also be built up into a number of levels. Between the pillars, 'balconies could be inserted', as necessary, and 'the back curtain could be changed . . . to give some variety of *décor*: dark curtains and pennants for *Hamlet*, highly-coloured, fairy-tale backgrounds for *All's Well that Ends Well*, and sunny vistas of light and air for *Twelfth Night*' (*ibid.*, p. xiv). For *King John*, a balcony was erected above the central arch, and it was here the citizens of Angiers appeared in Act II. In the court scenes, John's throne was placed centre stage. A brazier and chair created Arthur's dungeon, and, in the final scene, Swinstead Abbey was suggested by an illuminated cross which hung over the centre of the stage. Unfortunately, though the permanent setting appears to have been reasonably successful with regard to the remainder of the season's productions, the classical pillars and arches were considered to be a distraction in *King John*, particularly when contrasted with the 'too-authentic reproduction of the ugliest, heaviest and funniest armour in any period of medieval history' (Williamson, *Old Vic Drama*, 2, cited in Sprague, *Shakespeare's Histories*, p. 17). A number of critics deplored the ineffectiveness of the stylised battle scenes, *Plays and Players*, for example, commenting on the ludicrousness of 'a few faint breathless cries from the wings mingled with half a dozen supers putting steel to papier-mâché shields and trundling guns which look like the Charge of the Light Brigade' (vol. I, no. 3, December, 1953). Not infrequently, the audience laughed at the absurdity of it all. On 1 November, Ivor Brown, in *The Observer*, suggested that the 'military slash-and-scuffle' should be reduced. It was, anyway, unnecessary. 'Shakespeare's clangour of words makes battle-noise enough.'

The military clashes which provoked such hilarity were, in fact, a directorial addition. Onstage battle scenes occurred also in the nineteenth century, but they are not part of Shakespeare's play. In Shakespeare's text, onstage conflicts are entirely verbal, and the actual killing takes place off-stage. Characters strut and preen in front of the audience, as they hurl defiance at each other. They then exit to do battle and return, occasionally triumphant, but, more usually, battered and torn. In *King John* Shakespeare employs a mixture of dramatic styles, and it is difficult for a director to strike the appropriate note. What, for example, is an effective balance between the satirical perspective Shakespeare establishes with regard to the boastful prancing of the English and French kings, and the poignancy of the imprisoned Prince Arthur, or the tumult of Constance's grief? Is it better to seek an overall style which accommodates the various elements relatively seamlessley, or to stress their differentness? Nineteenth-century actor-managers saw the play as an animated slice of history, and, through a pageant-like reconstruction of the past, created a kind of cohesiveness, in which the audience were presented with a succession of constantly evolving moments of stilled stage action, rather like the pages of a story book. The battle scenes in the Old Vic production were ineffective partly because they did not fit into an overall conception of the play. Their bathos was not used to demonstrate the ridiculousness of the characters' bombastic utterances – an approach later taken, for example, by Buzz Goodbody in her 1970 Theatre-go-round production for the Royal Shakespeare Company.

Increasingly, stage design has been used in the twentieth century to embody visually the director's concept of the major unifying elements of the play. Audrey Cruddas's 1948 setting for *King John* worked in this way, its gradual disintegration mirroring the fate of John, and of England. Audrey Cruddas was again the designer for Douglas Seale's 1957 production for the Stratford Memorial Theatre. The single setting she created had, as its central feature, a squat, turreted, fortress-like structure. 'The imagery of war and violence which pervades the play was translated into terms of sinister, brooding atmosphere by setting the action either against a background of darkness or else an ominous leaden sky, shot with livid flame during the battle scenes' (Byrne, 'The Shakespeare season', p. 482). Throughout, the play 'glower[ed] like a low fire' (*Bolton Evening News*, 20 April) which, in the less sombre scenes, flamed into vivid life as the colourful costumes were caught in the bright pool of light which spilled on to the darkness. Douglas Seale brought the action downstage, close to the footlights, and dovetailed the scenes, so that the narrative was presented with great speed and vigour. In addition to the lighting, atmospheric music (by Christopher Whelen) was used to underscore the changes in mood. Most reviewers commented enthusiastically on the clarity and energy, especially of the first half. Any diminution of power in the second half was generally laid at Shakespeare's door.

Though the 1957 production was generally praised, the play, as so often, was found wanting. 'A rarely produced and rather patchy drama', observed the *South Wales Argus* (17 April) , 'the most indecisive of the histories' (*Wolverhampton Express and Star*, 17 April), and 'nobody's favourite play' (*Birmingham Mail*, 17 April). Nancy Banks-Smith, in the *Daily Herald*, quoted A. A. Milne: 'King John was not a good man / He had his little ways / Sometimes no-one spoke to him / For days and days and days' and added her own version: '*King John* is not a good play and sometimes no-one produces it for years' (17 April). The reasons why *King John* is 'not a good play' were the established ones. It is 'a play without a theme', Rosemary Anne Sisson explained in the *Stratford-upon-Avon Herald* (19 April), and 'it lacks a hero'. Both in 1953 and 1957 reviewers complained that the characters declaimed too much. In the *Daily Mail* of 28 October, 1953, Cecil Wilson began his account of the Old Vic production with the words: 'What the young English officer fresh from Dunkirk said of life on the beaches might equally be said of the play and its production: "The noise! And the people!"' In 1957, Rosemary Anne Sisson complained that 'No-one in *King John* ever speaks. They all declaim. Even little Arthur, pleading with Hubert, does so in piled imagery and antithesis, and Shakespeare had yet to learn such natural human dialogue as Henry uses with his soldiers in the night watches.' The effectiveness of the play in performance was generally attributed to the director. 'At Stratford Memorial Theatre you can see how a vigorous production and an outstanding performance lift a poor play out of the doldrums', the *Coventry Evening Telegraph* commented (17 April 1957). John's own deficiencies as a character were noted by a number of reviewers, Kenneth Tynan in *The Observer*, for example, dismissing him as 'a feeble waverer' (21 April 1957).

Above all, however, it was Constance who, in 1957, was considered to be the play's most problematic character: 'Chief wearer-out of welcomes is, of course, Constance, mother of little Arthur' (*Birmingham Mail*, 17 April); 'one can feel little but boredom for the excessive pleadings of Constance' (*Western Daily Press*, 20 April); 'one of the foremost of Shakespeare's gallery of wailing women' (*Birmingham Evening Despatch*, 17 April). Joan Miller's performance as Constance had its admirers. Rosemary Anne Sisson, for example, praised her 'superb Constance', whose 'railing never [became] tiresome, nor her grief tedious', and whose personal anguish made 'wars and treaties spring out of history and into life'. A more typical view was expressed, however, by the *Warwickshire Advertiser*: 'Amongst women of the play, Joan Miller makes a somewhat tiresome figure of grief out of Constance' (19 April).

Finding a style for Constance
Variations in critical opinion clearly must reflect the personal preferences of the individual reviewer, but they also reflect, in their diverse ways, the beliefs of a particular period as to what constitutes good theatre. Constance has been seen as problematic in the twentieth century because she conveys an intensity of grief through language that is formalised to a very high degree. *The Birmingham Post* reviewer in 1957 defined the difficulty as being that Constance's railing and 'magnificent lamentations' need 'a Siddons attack' (17 April). In 1953 reviewers generally praised Fay Compton as Constance, *Plays and Players*, for example, describing her performance as 'great' and 'tragic', and *The Observer* commenting that she had 'authentic power and immense pathos'. On this occasion too, however, her performance was compared with that of Mrs Siddons, not

entirely favourably. After noting that *King John* was 'a favourite sounding-board for the rhetorical acting of the eighteenth century', Ivor Brown, in *The Observer*, went on to describe how Sarah Siddons 'following Mrs. Cibber made Constance one of her "lift the roof and set-'em-fainting" parts and now we have Fay Compton in grand vocal form to scream, like Bellona in full blast, against a patched-up peace and to pour lamentation over little Arthur lost'. He criticised the director for taking an interval after Act II, with the result that Fay Compton was given no build-up for her 'Gone to be married?' speech, and related the story of Sarah Siddons working herself into a passion as she sat offstage listening as the French king reneged on his promises to her. Fay Compton had, by contrast, to wait while the audience went for 'chatter, coffee and cake' and had then to pour 'out the Queen's fury to returning listeners who have probably forgotten what it's all about'. W. A. Darlington in *The Daily Telegraph* also criticised the placing of the interval, and blamed this for a lessening of the power of Fay Compton's performance in III.i. In addition, though commenting that she acted Constance as well as any actress he had seen in the part, he felt that 'somehow the Siddons touch escapes our modern actresses'.

Sarah Siddons herself, however, seemed dated to some commentators by the end of the nineteenth century, and, in the twentieth, actresses have had immense difficulty in finding an acceptable performance style for Constance's highly patterned language. The *News Chronicle* of 17 April 1957, found Joan Miller's manner 'homely rather than grand' and *The Daily Telegraph* was of the view that she 'conveyed little more [in III.i] than that she was rather cross' (17 April). Richard David commented: 'The part of Constance in *King John* is full of, is altogether constructed out of, elaborate patterns of language, the balances and contrasts and repetitions of set rhetoric. To superimpose on this formal presentation of tragedy the sobs, the shrieks, the incessantly quivering hands of a real-life hysteric (as did Joan Miller at Stratford in 1957) is to set form against content. You cannot create a part by two incompatible methods of presentation employed simultaneously' ('Actors and scholars', p. 84).

A performance style for Constance with which a twentieth-century audience can identify, while, at the same time, not perceiving her heightened language as somehow dislocated from the character, is undeniably hard to find. The frequency with which words such as 'ranting' 'railing' 'tiresome' and 'wailing' are used in reviews points, however, to a lack of sympathy which is essentially connected with the *character*, rather than the actress. Even those reviewers who praised Joan Miller's performance did so in terms of the 'great tact' she showed with Constance's 'songs of sorrow' (*Yorkshire Post*, 17 April 1957), or the skill whereby her railing never became 'tiresome, not her grief tedious' (*Stratford-upon-Avon Herald*). It is difficult when reading repeated criticisms of Constance's tiresomeness to escape the view that what it is really tiresome about her is precisely the vehemence of her anger. After all, despite the successes of such actresses as Mrs Cibber and Sarah Siddons, a certain embarrassment, or, at least, lack of sympathy, with Constance's anger has a long history. Colley Cibber clearly found it difficult to cope with, and so, in his version, every time Constance expresses anger, she immediately suppresses it. In the last scene, she even reappears to forgive John after attending her child's funeral. Sarah Siddons's central concept of the character as 'a lofty and proud spirit, associated with the most exquisite feelings of maternal tenderness' (Campbell, *Life of Mrs Siddons*, quoted in Waith, '*King John* and the drama of history', p. 198), clearly worked well in its time, but the development of more intimate theatres and performance styles, alongside a certain distaste for 'lofty' pride, and probably 'exquisite feelings of maternal tenderness' as well, has made life difficult for the actress. It is instructive, therefore, to return to Shakespeare's text and read his depiction of Constance's anger and grief in III.iv (a scene which, in the twentieth century, has often been seen as problematic). The language is undeniably repetitive and highly formalised, but what comes through, above all, is the *impotence* of Constance's anger. When Philip, the King of France, tells her to have peace, she turns on him with the words:

No, no, I will not, having breath to cry!
O that my tongue were in the thunder's mouth!
Then with a passion would I shake the world,
And rouse from sleep that fell anatomy
Which cannot hear a lady's feeble voice,
Which scorns a modern invocation. (III.iv.37–42)

However much Constance rants and rails, her voice remains the 'feeble voice' of a woman. The king who tells her to be peaceful has betrayed her to the enemy after promising to place her child on the English throne, to which he has as strong a claim, or stronger, than John. Pandulph, the calculating politician, tells Constance she holds 'too heinous a respect of grief', and the angry helpless mother rejoins: 'He talks to me that never had a son.' The superb thing about this scene is surely precisely the fact that Shakespeare understood that anger is a vital component of grief (and so, if biographical detail is valuable in dating the play, then perhaps Hamnet Shakespeare's year of death *is* relevant). He understood, too, the helplessness of Constance as a woman. After her scathing reply to Pandulph, King Philip accuses her of being as fond of grief as she is of her son. Her answering speech beginning 'Grief fills the room up of my absent child' is rightly considered one of the most beautiful and moving pieces of writing of the whole play, but it is also Constance's justification for the constant repetitions that Pandulph, Philip and many later commentators on the play have found so wearying. Her child has been captured, and will, almost certainly, be murdered. Have I not, she asks the Machiavell and the traitor, 'reason to be fond of grief?'

John and the Bastard
Apart from the playing of Constance, critical comments on the acting, both in 1953 and in 1957, focused chiefly on the roles of John and the Bastard. In 1953, Philip Hope-Wallace in *The Manchester Guardian* praised Richard Burton's 'gleaming eye and . . . bold masculine effrontery' as the Bastard (28 October), and *The Times* commented that he gave 'the whimsically ob-servant Bastard some of that silent momentousness which Sir

Laurence Olivier once gave to Hotspur. Even when silent among the bawling barons he rivets attention and when it is his turn to act as chorus to the action he catches the blunt humour of the man' (28 October). Michael Hordern's King John was also highly commended, though a number of reviewers expressed dissatisfaction with the character. *The Manchester Guardian*, for example, was of the opinion that the Bastard was 'the only live part in this pungent pageant; the hero-king has to be made up as he goes along', and *The Observer* considered that John was a character about whom Shakespeare had come to no definite conclusion. He was 'at once the ringing voice of Protestant Tudorism and the disgraceful example of power abused'. For *The Times* reviewer, Michael Hordern's John was 'an opportunist of near genius'. He made 'the movement of that intensely political mind an interesting spectacle', and so helped the audience to understand the Bastard's loyalty. Unsatisfactory king as John undoubtedly was in many ways, in the context of the internal and external dangers facing the country, he was an 'entirely adequate symbol of kingship'. Even in the final scene, 'hunted, haunted . . . wracked equally with terror and remorse', Hordern was recognisably a king, and 'in death his features seemed to assume the cast of some medieval effigy from Westminster Abbey' (Wood and Clarke, p. 63), thus effectively underlining the rightness of the Bastard's decision to be faithful to him.

In 1957 reviewers again commented on both John's inconsistency and the investiture of the character by the actor, Robert Harris, with attributes that justified the Bastard's loyalty. The *Oxford Times* of 19 April noted that, despite John's ruthlessness and cynicism, he displayed a 'compelling kingliness', while Rosemary Anne Sisson observed that, throughout his performance, Robert Harris conveyed 'a sense of the divinity which hedges even a usurping King'. Alec Clunes as the Bastard was highly praised by a number of reviewers. The *Yorkshire Post* considered his interpretation 'a definitive one', and J. C. Trewin, in an article entitled 'Happy returns', wrote, 'Alec Clunes is now the voice of England: I cannot imagine the part invested with more authority and character'. In the opinion of the *Oxford*

Times reviewer, Clunes's 'mixture of poetry, wit and masculine grace [was] one of the brightest jewels to have adorned the crown of Stratford acting for many years'. Something of a question mark is perhaps raised against Clunes's performance, however, by the terms of the *Daily Mail*'s commendation: 'I have seen bluffer and subtler Bastards, but few better looking or nobler-voiced' (17 April). Kenneth Tynan in *The Observer*, more forthrightly, commented that Alec Clunes transformed 'the madcap Bastard into a hearty, beaming clergyman summoned to restore order to an unruly youth club'. For Tynan, it was Robert Harris's John that was the play's 'emotional centre'.

Muriel St Clare Byrne also praised Robert Harris's performance, for its 'profound fidelity to the Elizabethan play which Shakespeare wrote' ('The Shakespeare season', p. 484). Drawing on a school of mid-twentieth-century critical thought which viewed *King John*, like the other English history plays, as reflective of Elizabethan political structures and ideology, she developed a line of argument which discounted the Bastard as the play's hero. 'As I see it', she wrote, '*King John* is a theme without heroes, but with spokesmen. The theme is the interdependence of Tudor nationalism and internal unity.' However, 'the material is dramatically recalcitrant, and the author is reduced to forcing a card on us' (*ibid.*, p. 483). She divided the character of John into three distinct units. Firstly, there was 'a build-up of the Tudor "Reformation hero" derived from Holinshed, Bale and *The Troublesome Reign*, combined with a build-up of the Monarch as the spokesman or symbol of Tudor nationalism'. At the heart of the play was Shakespeare's exploration of the 'evil, cruel, unscrupulous and unstable' John, 'a highly dramatic use of historical truth, as seen by John's contemporaries and by the later historian, but ignored by Tudor writers'. In the final section, by a sleight of hand, 'the royal *mystique*' was nominally rehabilitated. With Arthur dead, John became the legitimate king, and he gained additional sympathy because Shakespeare attributes the revolt of the barons 'not to his tyrannous rule but to the death of Arthur, of which he was not guilty in fact . . . and for which he is allowed at least some show of repentance' (*ibid.*). The Bastard's role in the latter part of the play Byrne saw as being to speak on behalf of the 'national theme' and to 'make the Monarch the rallying point for national unity' when, in V.ii, he defies Pandulph on John's behalf. Alec Clunes's performance she found 'light-weight', and she also castigated his subdued rendering of the Bastard's final 'ringing' words (*ibid.*, p. 484).

Though Alec Clunes depicted the Bastard as an heroic figure, his interpretation of the end of the play prefigured (as did Anthony Quayle's quiet, reflective speaking of the lines in 1948) the more radical questioning of patriotism – and of heroism – in John Barton's 1974 and 1975 adaptations of *King John* and Deborah Warner's 1988/89 production.

CHAPTER IV

Royal Shakespeare Company productions of the 1970s

Between 1970 and 1975 the Royal Shakespeare Company presented three versions of *King John*: the 1970 Theatre-go-round production directed by Buzz Goodbody, and John Barton's 1974 and 1975 adaptations, none of which sympathised with a reading of the play which validated such concepts as 'royal *mystique*' or the interdependence of nationalism and internal unity. In their different ways, both Goodbody and Barton stressed instead the inherently corrupt nature of politicians and power structures. Like Colley Cibber two hundred years earlier, John Barton used Shakespeare's text as a springboard to create his own play, which he believed to be more relevant to the contemporary world. Buzz Goodbody's simplified, pared-down touring version, which played schools, colleges and community centres in addition to the Royal Shakespeare Theatre, was both childlike and satiric, a combination of A. A. Milne and *Ubu Roi*.

Milne, in fact, featured in a number of the reviews of the Theatre-go-round production. Like Nancy Banks-Smith in her account of Douglas Seale's 1957 production in the *Daily Herald*, Benedict Nightingale in the *New Statesman* quoted Milne's poem about King John and suggested, in addition, that the inspiration for Patrick Stewart's John was 'a sort of perverted Tigger; a malicious, gleeful, bouncing child who, unfortunately, is in a position to pull wings off people as well as flies'. In this, moreover, he was at one with a world in which 'War is a hilarious trip to the seaside, and [the nobles] giggle and nudge one another as they prepare to knock down the sandcastles of Angiers. Push, kick, stamp, and then back home for tea' (19 June 1970). Peter Thomson described John's 'whooping rocking-horse gallop round the stage', following his order for the march on Calais (III.iii.73), and his farcical death, in the course of which he slid rigidly from the throne to the floor and his golden cushion fell with 'a gentle plop' on to his face ('A necessary theatre', p. 118). It was, Thomson thought, 'a pity that this production of *King John* took place at all. Its flippancy was ill-judged and often puerile. Buzz Goodbody . . . imposed on [the play] a single simplified view of politics as a dangerous game incompetently played by caricature kings and councillors who can give or take a giggle but defy respect' (*ibid.*, p. 117). Somehow, the pathos of the Hubert/Arthur scene survived this trivialising approach, but, in Act II, Sheila Burrell as Constance had no choice but to overstretch her voice, given the general hilarity of the proceedings, and Norman Rodway, as the Bastard, was made redundant by the director's insistence 'that *she*, not *he*, should expose the "Mad world! mad kings! mad composition!"' Perhaps the saddest thing about the production, Peter Thomson suggested, was that it ended up not as 'a parody of the business of politics' but as 'a parody of the business of acting'. When 'actors "pass over the stage" for laughs or form in straight downstage lines, facing front, to speak their words as foolishness', it is not 'politicians who are mocked' but the 'theatrical profession' (*ibid.*, p. 118).

Some of the newspaper reviews, however, were more favourable. The *Coventry Evening Telegraph* noted the appositeness of presenting a play which is 'utterly cynical about national politics' during a General Election campaign (11 June 1970), and the *Northampton Chronicle and Echo* applauded the decision to turn *King John* 'into a pageant of spirited fun, rather than a tragic, fervid melodrama' (12 June). Hilary Spurling in the *Spectator* was particularly enthusiastic. Unlike Benedict Nightingale, who thought that audiences could not hoot with laughter one moment 'and mourn the next, switching from pantomime to

[63]

graveyard', Spurling commented that the deliberate artificiality of the performance style both reflected '*King John*'s often weirdly euphuistic rhetoric' and suited 'to admiration the play's abrupt transitions from tragedy to horse laughs' (19 June). This was a bold, intelligent production which, once the 'historical pageantry and patriotic fervour, both tacked on in the nineteenth century and both equally foreign' to the play, were removed, revealed a ghoulish, cartoon-like text, consisting 'largely of grand guignol violence', in which entire armies are 'boisterously slaughtered between one line and the next'. It was also a text, however, which, in Spurling's view, 'only intermittently' touched 'the depths of Shakespeare's later histories'.

John Barton's *King John*, Stratford-upon-Avon, 1974, and London, 1975

On 20 March 1974 a production of *King John* opened at the Royal Shakespeare Theatre in Stratford. The direction was by John Barton, with Barry Kyle. To a substantial degree the author was also John Barton, a fact attested by Michael Billington's observation in *The Guardian*: 'This must be the first time in history the Stratford-on-Avon festival has opened with a new play' (21 March 1974), and the following extract from Robert Cushman's review for *The Observer* (24 March 1974): 'This year's season at Stratford on Avon began on Wednesday with William Shakespeare's *King John*. So, at least, declared the programme, thereby exposing the Royal Shakespeare Company not merely to criticism, but to possible prosecution under the Trades Descriptions Act.'

The vexed question of authorship had been clarified when the production transferred to the Aldwych Theatre, London, the following January, the piece being described in the programme as adapted and reworked by John Barton from Shakespeare's *King John* and other sources. Both the 1974 and 1975 programmes included notes by the adaptor-director explaining the reasons for the changes he had made. Barton's 1974 programme statement included the following words:

Whenever I have seen *King John* on the stage I have been fascinated yet perplexed. When I read it again at the end of 1973, I was struck by how much the play, probably written in 1594, is about England and us *now* . . . Even the specific political issues have modern parallels, although I have never seen this emerge fully in performance. So I turned to *The Troublesome Reign of King John* (Shakespeare's probable source-play, 1591) and to the Tudor *King Johan* (1539) for clues as to why.

I found that those areas left cloudy by *King John* were more clearly explored in *The Troublesome Reign* . . . It appeared that a marriage of the two texts might be fruitful.

In 1975, Barton identified the areas of obscurity in Shakespeare's play, and pointed to elements in the text which had served as the basis for his revision of *King John*.

Shakespeare's *King John*, as critics and scholars have recognised, is a very uneven piece of work. It raises questions and expectations which it does not pursue; it does not explore potentially interesting characters (especially King John himself); and it leaves crucial events (like John's second coronation) unexplained. It also has elements of a vital, bold, Morality play style, but this is submerged under the sometimes overweighted and overteeming rhetoric of the style Shakespeare has chosen. I decided therefore to rework the text and incorporate passages from the earlier plays.

Throughout the adaptation process Barton's intention was 'not so much to improve a rich but flawed piece of work, as to make it more accessible'. The cutting and transposition of Shakespeare's text, the additions from varied sources, and the interpolation of visual action intended to illustrate and clarify the narrative – all these alterations were made in order to render more available to an audience a play which was perceived as incoherent and obscure. Prior to its transfer to London, the production underwent further adaptation in the course of which a number of lines which drew parallels with the contemporary state of England (notably 'the price of goods / Soars meteor-like into the louring heavens / Whiles that our purses dwindle and decline', a Bartonesque addition which was greeted caustically by a number of reviewers) were deleted. By contrast with the 1974 version, the 1975 production appears to have been tighter and more coherent, a newly-devised prologue establishing from the onset the 'Morality play style' of the piece.

The version of *King John* which opened at the Royal Shakespeare Theatre in March 1974 consisted of '2,595 lines . . . something like 1,350 . . . [of which] were more or less recognizably based on Shakespeare's play, though many of these were altered or redistributed' (Smallwood, 'Shakespeare unbalanced', p. 83). In place of Shakespeare's abrupt immersion of his audience in the Anglo-French quarrel, the performance began with a prologue in which Richard I's will was read, naming John as his successor and revoking a previous will in Arthur's favour. This was followed at the start of the first of the nineteen scenes by Eleanor's presentation of her son to the assembled barons and then by John's coronation. It was only after this ceremony that the interchange between John and Chatillon (here changed to Melun) which opens Shakespeare's play got under way. Scene ii offered a mirror image of events in the prologue and the opening of scene i, Constance presenting her son as England's king and citing a will as evidence.

> Arthur, my son that must by lawful right
> Succeed his uncle Richard to the throne
> Of England: 'tis his true inheritance,
> Attested here by Cordelion's will.

Richard's earlier will, which pronounced John 'unfit for rule' and bequeathed the kingdom to Arthur, was then read, and Arthur, in the same voluminous gold cloak that his uncle had worn, was crowned in his turn. Clearly, the purpose of these additional sequences was to spell out for an audience the basic question which motivates the action of *King John*: who is the legitimate king of England? Vital background information *is* given in Shakespeare's play. Soon after the beginning Eleanor privately reminds her son of the shaky basis of his rule: 'Your strong possession much more than your right / Or else it must go wrong with you and me' (I.i.40–1), and, in Act II, after identifying Arthur as the legitimate heir because he is the child of John's elder brother, King Philip asks John: 'In the name of God / How comes it then that thou art called king . . . ?'(II.i.106–7).

It is possible, however, that, in the quick-fire opening of the play, the significance of Eleanor's words could be missed, and the static nature of Act II can result in the details of the competing claims of the various contenders for power being lost. It is perhaps not surprising, therefore, that the director should have felt a need to explain the historical background upon which John's and Arthur's claims to the throne were based. The chronological inversion of the two wills can also be seen as introducing a note of irony from the start of the performance, the power and ceremony of a king being revealed as dependent on the changing whim of the previous incumbent of the throne. Had Richard lived, he might well have changed his will again. There is, however, a difficulty attendant on clarifying what Shakespeare left ambiguous – or obscure, depending on one's point of view – and that is that a John seen ascending the throne as a consequence of his predecessor's finally expressed intention – however arbitrary that decision is later shown to be – becomes, technically at least, legitimate. Power itself may be revealed as being based on the rockiest of foundations; but John, nevertheless, within the established conventions of the transfer of that power, is shown as having a stronger right than Arthur.

The fact that the presentation of parallel wills and coronations was meant to establish from the outset the corrupt nature of the power over which the various contenders squabbled was shown by the extension of these devices as a patterning element throughout the piece as a whole. In total, six coronations were shown, one each for Arthur, Henry and Lewis (who was crowned by the English lords in the scene equivalent to Shakespeare's V.ii), and three for John who was twice recrowned, in scenes corresponding to Shakespeare's IV.ii and V.i. For each ceremony, except John's third coronation, the same gold cloak was used, thus stressing the interchangeability of the various candidates for power. John's final coronation – by Pandulph (Jeffery Dench), wearing what Irving Wardle termed 'a sarcophagus-like robe' (*The Times*, 21 March 1974), with an enormously high metal collar – was staged as a nightmarish parody of the other five investitures. Instead of being clothed in gold, John was stripped to a loin-cloth and made to kiss Pandulph's boot as a gesture of submission, 'crowned with a dunce's cap and pushed onto the throne to hold a skull and bone in place of the orb and sceptre which figured in all the other ceremonies. The ceremony was completed with the old music-hall routine of a custard-pie in the face' (Smallwood, 'Shakespeare unbalanced', p. 90). Richard's two wills which initiated the contest over the crown found their parallel in John's attempt to name his own successor. In the penultimate scene Hubert told the Bastard about a will John had made, its purpose being 'To change a will'. Like his eldest brother, John, in his final testament, attempted to bequeath the kingdom away from his young heir. When the Bastard read the contents of the will aloud later, however, he named Henry as John's successor, though with a telling pause before the prince's name. In the 1975 production Henry's subsequent coronation was temporarily halted because the crown had been lost in the Wash. Observing that they should 'not bate one jot of ceremony', the Bastard improvised a new crown by tearing up John's will, revealing both the limitation and the absurdity of kingly power through one childish image. In the Barton *King John* there was no concluding moment of hope. The optimism of Shakespeare's final lines was undercut by the fact that they were not the Bastard's personal statement on the present and future state of England. Instead, they were distanced and put into question by the fact that the Bastard read them from a book, scarcely raising his eyes from the page as he did so. Offstage, the French forces were preparing for war, Pandulph's peace initiatives (in contrast to those of his Shakespearean counterpart) rejected.

The inherent tendency of power to corrupt all who touched it, even the innocent, was emphasised in the 1975 production through a paralleling of John and Arthur, which was effected through rewriting the Hubert/Arthur scene and adding material to Arthur's speeches as he attempted to escape from his prison. In the new Hubert/Arthur scene, Hubert entered reading a book about King Arthur, and this led to a discussion with his

[68]

prisoner on the nature of King Arthur and whether, as some people believed, he could be still living. If he were alive, Prince Arthur asked, what would he do? – to which Hubert replied: 'Speak true, and be no boggler.' This reference to King Arthur would seem to have had a twofold function. Firstly, it was a means of introducing the notion of the true king, a development which enabled Arthur to ask Hubert who his king was, and for Hubert, consequently, to face up to the dilemma of whether or not he would carry out his promise to John. Secondly, it served to link the 'little prince' with his legendary namesake, and thereby to confer on him a measure of authority which he otherwise lacked. As always, however, in the Barton *John*, authority was suspect. Before attempting his escape in the next scene but one, Arthur explained the reason for his action, his anxiety that Hubert might repent of his decision to be merciful. Despite his fear of the danger that awaited him, he would 'venture it / To win a Kingdom'. When his escape bid resulted in fatal injury, he blamed himself, claiming that he was justly punished because he had dreamed that he was a king.

> Alack, men clamour'd forth *Vive le Roy*
> To one that was a little vaunting boy,
> That would have been a King, but knew not how.

In this version of *King John* even dreams of power resulted in destruction. Little Arthur's connection with the story-book king spelled death. Ironically, however, the boy who, in life, did not know how to be a king achieved this status through his death. In the next scene, John described himself as 'a little king, a sneaping king', diminutive and childish like Arthur, except that, by dying, Arthur had taken hold of men's minds.

> And little Arthur now, that lies in mould,
> Is greater, being graven in memory,
> Than he that half-lives yet, this little John.

The interconnection of Arthur and John was additional to certain parallels that Shakespeare himself employs, notably between Hubert and the Bastard in the later scenes of the play, when, in contrast to virtually all the other characters, they

[69]

attempt to behave honourably. In the Barton *King John* Hubert was further linked both, briefly, with Melun, and, more extensively, in 1974, with the twin characters of Peter of Pomfret and First Monk, and, in 1975, a new character Death, the Presenter, who was an amalgamation of the two. (In both productions the roles were played by Mike Gwilym.) In 1975, scenes xiv and xv each consisted of a monologue, the first by Hubert, the second by Melun, with the result that an admission by Hubert that he would like to leave John, but 'none would take [him] up' was followed by Melun's revelation of Lewis's treacherous intentions towards the English lords. Hubert's defection, though desired, was not achieved. Instead, he formed the intention of taking John into the nearby Swinstead Abbey, 'Where it is said they heal the sick in mind'. Played by David Suchet with a 'savage birth-mark across one eye and cheek [which] belonged to a child's nightmare, and made more notable Arthur's trust in him' (Thomson, 'The smallest season', p. 140), Hubert was portrayed as a separate character from the Citizen of Angiers and was present from the first scene. Irving Wardle described his relationship with John as that of 'a Horatio-like confidant' (*The Times*, 21 March 1974), a role to which Mike Gwilym's character acted as a kind of sinister double. In 1974 Richard I's will in John's favour was read by the First Monk. For the 1975 production, a new prologue by John Barton dispensed with this will, and in its place Death, the Presenter, introduced himself, and the play, to the audience.

> Gentles, perchance you know me not
> > A fellow I am of fame;
> I am that king whereof they sing
> > But I tell you not my name.
> . . .
> Now, gentles, must our game begin;
> > Therefore be merry, all;
> Remember well what I you tell,
> > And come when I you call.

In Shakespeare's play, Peter of Pomfret appears once and speaks one line only (IV.ii.154). In the Barton *John* this was expanded, so that, as in *The Troublesome Reign*, he interpreted for the king the significance of the premonitory signs that are reported as having been seen in the heavens. In the Ascension Day scene (V.i), in which, in Shakespeare's version, John has in fact not realised that the day has arrived on which Peter prophesied he would give up his crown, Peter of Pomfret was led onstage by John who was holding him by a noose tied round his neck. When Peter refused to do the king's bidding and 'unsay' his prophecy, John commanded that he should be hanged. Peter's warning: 'ere this year's end and we shall see again', and John's response: 'Belike, belike and sing a carol too / At Christmastide, and dance beside the fire' prepared for a scene which has no counterpart in Shakespeare's play, the poisoning of John by the First Monk/Death.

This scene (xvii) was set first outside and then within Swinstead Abbey at Christmas-time. In words which partially echoed Arthur's dying realisation that his dream of greatness had been the literal cause of his downfall, John referred to his previous night's dream that he 'was no more a King'. The sound of carol singing coming from the Abbey caused him to reflect that this was the night on which 'our blissful Saviour / Took mortal mould', the same night on which the 'wretched' John was born. The bringing together of John's dream, presumably signifying his death, and Christ's and his own nativity was followed, in the abbey, by a winter enactment of a kind of Last Supper, with John seated at a long table in the centre of twelve cowled monks. In the context of this reference to Christian iconography, the earlier image of John stripped of his garments and crowned with a dunce's cap became a version of the scourging of Christ and his crowning with thorns. Among the hooded monks at the Last Supper were Hubert and the First Monk/ Death. In 1975 the latter's function to act first as a memento mori, and then as a death-bringer, in opposition to Hubert who, apart from his refusal to carry out the king's orders by blinding Arthur, remained loyal to John, was made clear when Hubert pleaded with John to drink from a bowl *he* had tasted, and not the one his guests were offering him. A photograph of this scene by Donald Cooper shows the linked, but antithetical roles played by David Suchet and Mike Gwilym. John (Emrys James) was seated at the table. Behind him (stage left) David Suchet, his scarred faced turned towards the camera, had just placed the bowl in front of the king. Emrys James held David Suchet's arm restrainingly, while, at the same time, tenderly laying his head against it. To his right, and, again from behind, Mike Gwilym aggressively thrust towards him a poisoned bowl. In an earlier soliloquy he had explained to the audience the reason for his choice of poison as the means of John's death. People had suggested a variety of other weapons, but he had decided on poison as being the most fitting because John was 'a poison / To England's earth and all this famous land'.

Both the 1974 and 1975 productions stressed the omnipresence of death in the midst of life and the essentially corrupt nature of power. After the grotesque coronation ceremony in scene xii (V.i), Pandulph identified the crown as the source of John's downfall, and reminded characters and audience of their precarious hold on life.

> Within this circle is thy wretched story.
> I charge all men that sitteth here in hall,
> Think well upon the history of John:
> For though you live in lust and liking all,
> Your flesh, as his corrupt, will fade anon:
> For flesh, the soul's thin garment, is but lent
> To mortal man: therefore be penitent.

The performance style of both productions was presentational, lines being redistributed and reallocated, so that a number of characters had at points a choric function. In 1974, for example, Eleanor's rebuke to her son because his mishandling of the 'ambitious Constance' would now result in war with France (I.i.35–8) was spoken by Salisbury, so that it became part of the background information which was offered to the audience. After the interval, in 1975, John brought the audience up to date by detailing for them Constance's death, Arthur's imprisonment and his own problems with the Pope. The Bastard's role as commentator was developed by altering the position of lines 350–60 (II.i) so that they became a soliloquy, his description of death 'mousing the flesh of men / In undetermined differences of kings' thus referring to the battle taking place offstage; and, in 1975, inserting an additional speech explaining to the audience the dilemma he found himself in after Arthur's death: 'I have sworn allegiance to a corrupted King / And now belike I am myself corrupt.' Blanche's speech beginning 'The sun's o'ercast with blood' (III.i.326–336), in which she comes to the realisation that whichever side wins the battle (her uncle's or her husband's) she will be the loser, became the final speech of the corresponding scene in the Barton version. Her premonitory vision of a blood-soaked and increasingly fragmented world therefore came after John's statement that only 'the dearest-valued blood, of France' could allay his rage and demonstrated the pointlessness of the Anglo-French war which was about to recommence in earnest. Her line: 'There where my fortune lives, there my life dies' was changed to: 'Yet if our fortune thrives, my England dies', thus adding to the sense of hopelessness and emphasising the destructiveness of personal ambition.

Throughout, England was presented as battered and maimed by the self-interested actions of those in power. Melun's 1975 soliloquy (scene xv, Shakespeare's V.iv), ended with a plea to the English lords: 'By Christ's sweet blood, be not your country's bane / Where be you now? Come home, come home again!' In the next scene but one (the poisoning scene) John sang a carol which began: 'Come home again', and went on to tell of the red blood shed by Christ. It ended with the final words of Death's Prologue: 'Remember well / What I you tell / And come when I you call', so equating home / England with the grave. All of Shakespeare's lines for Prince Henry were redistributed (the Mike Gwilym character speaking the words 'What surety of the world, what hope, what stay / When this was now a king, and now is clay?' V.vii.68–9). Henry's only, interpolated, speech was a plea that those present should 'for the love of God, look to the state of England'. Christopher Hudson's description of Henry in the *Evening Standard*, however (21 March 1974) –

'Gold-masked like a puppet, he comes hopelessly to the front of the stage' – hardly suggests that his words are likely to lead to very positive results. The bleakness of the conclusion was underlined by the offstage approach of the French forces, and the Bastard's assessment of the future state of England. 'Now must thou rule this isle, and no man here / Knows how thou mayst.' The decision, in 1975, to use the same actor in the roles of both Prince Arthur and Prince Henry further reinforced this pessimistic outcome. A resurrected image of the dead victim of past power battles offered little hope of a constructive use of power in the future.

Critical responses

Two articles, Peter Thomson's 'The smallest season: the Royal Shakespeare Company at Stratford in 1974', and R. L. Smallwood's 'Shakespeare unbalanced: the Royal Shakespeare Company's *King John*, 1974–5', are particularly valuable in the detailed critical response they offer on the Barton *King John*. The former concentrates exclusively, the latter primarily, on the 1974 version. Peter Thomson makes it clear that he is not opposed in principle to adaptations of Shakespeare's work, but contrasts the approach of 'a Marowitz, who leaves the original text where it is and then composes a critical exploration of it' ('The smallest season', p. 138) with Barton's restructurings and emendations which, in his view, irremediably altered Shakespeare's play (and, despite the explanatory programme notes, a Stratford audience would assume that what they were seeing was by Shakespeare). A 'fascinating' and 'unruly original' had been pruned and simplified to turn it 'into a well-made play' (*ibid.*), expressive of Barton's, not Shakespeare's, views on the nature of power. The visual embodiment of that power – the golden coronation cloak – Thomson identifies as the one used also in John Barton's productions of *Richard II* and *Cymbeline* (both part of the current Stratford season). 'It is a vivid costume item designed to reinforce the notion of the king's two bodies by diminishing the *man* who dares to wear it; but determination to use it in plays so dissimilar does also suggest the super-imposition of a directorial idea that pre-dates a new encounter with each text' (*ibid.*, p. 139).

The frequent religious references, which have few counterparts in Shakespeare's play, Thomson sees as further evidence of a misplaced focus of attention. 'Barton was listening to himself rather than to the play' (*ibid.*, p. 141). With regard to the performances, he particularly commends David Suchet as Hubert, and comments favourably on Sheila Allen's Constance, and Salisbury (Denis Holmes) 'holding his counsel like a wise uncle' (*ibid.*, p. 140). The directorial interpretation of the Bastard, however, defeated the normally 'excellent' Richard Pasco, and Emrys James was 'a nursery king, a mother's boy without an inkling of adult responsibility' (*ibid.*, p. 139), whose tendency, in the first three acts at least, to rely on easy laughs cheapened the play. The most serious example of this, in Thomson's view, occurred in III.i when Pandulph enquired of John: 'Why thou against the church, our holy mother / So wilfully dost spurn; and force preforce / Keep Stephen Langton' (III.i.141–3), and was interrupted at this point by 'John's by-play of ignorance' (p. 139) as to the identity of Stephen Langton. This piece of business, Thomson argues, deprived John of any rightful claim to the Bastard's 'company, Hubert's love, or the enmity of France and Rome' (*ibid.*, p. 140). A king who does not know the name of his designated archbishop of Canterbury, 'or who pretends not to know (and how are *we* to distinguish?)' (*ibid.*) is too slight and inconsequential a figure to be worthy of concern. John's own insubstantiality was symptomatic of the production as a whole. If such a major adaptation of Shakespeare's text was really considered necessary, Thomson though that it would have been wiser to have found a more able dramatist than John Barton to undertake the task. If John's reign was to be subjected to contemporary scrutiny, this could have been achieved by pairing *King John* with a twentieth-century play. The obvious choice, Arden's *Left-Handed Liberty*, was problematic because of the RSC's recent dispute with Arden. This 'kind of juxtaposition' could, however, valuably be more fully 'investigated' (*ibid.*, p. 141).

Smallwood's article examines the problems inherent in John Barton's decision to 'develop and clarify tendencies already present in the three plays' (1974 programme note) from which his *John* was fashioned, in the light of Barton's 1975 statement that his aim was to make the production 'more accessible'. Arguing that 'the man who joins together what Shakespeare left asunder and attempts simultaneously to produce three plays for the price of one is in serious danger of losing the individual focus of them all in a general blur' ('Shakespeare unbalanced', p. 82), Smallwood analyses the supposed 'accessibility' of the Barton adaptations. He applauds the decision to present Hubert as a separate character from that of the Citizen of Angiers, and to show him in attendance on John from the beginning, finding particularly effective the scene in which John, 'weary after battle' (*ibid.*, p. 84) was massaged by Hubert as he gradually broached the subject of Arthur's death. The incorporation of the various wills, however, far from acting as a source of clarification, Smallwood considers confusing, in contrast with Shakespeare's use of Eleanor's lines (I.i.40–1) which so effectively and economically establish the dubious nature of John's right to the crown. Barton's fleshing-out of John's quarrel with Rome and the addition of the poisoning scene had the effect of muddying further the clarity of focus in Shakespeare's text. With the exception of John's outburst in III.i, Shakespeare deliberately avoids the anti-Catholic polemic of *The Troublesome Reign*, and makes few religious allusions, with the result that he is able to concentrate instead 'on political questions as they affect personal morality' (*ibid.*, p. 87), especially in relation to the choices Hubert and the Bastard must face in the final two acts of the play. While John's defiance of Rome in *The Troublesome Reign* makes sense within the prevailing religious and political context of Shakespeare's day, members of a present-day audience are hardly likely to view events from the perspective of their sixteenth-century counterparts. The religious element of the Barton *John* was also bewildering because it conflicted with Emrys James's portrayal of John as, in the main, 'corrupt and comic' (*ibid.*, p. 88), and with the production's underlying assumption of the corruptibility of power and 'the futility of existence, given the inevitability of death' (*ibid.*, p. 89). This latter 'morality-play' element Smallwood sees as lacking in substance because, like the absence of a context for the anti-Roman invective, the vital ingredient of 'religious faith' which would render the morality 'meaningful' was missing. 'Mr Barton presented the trappings without the heart of the plays' (*ibid.*, p. 93). The attempt to establish topical parallels between the corrupt state of England depicted in Shakespeare's play and current debates over entry into Europe and the spiralling cost of living Smallwood considers misguided. The 'Commodity' speech was both cut and distended to include an unnecessary further gloss on the Bastard's analysis of the prevalence of self-interest –

> That smooth-fac'd gentleman, Commodity,
> Or in your vulgar, thus: Expedience,
> Self-Interest, Policy, the Common Weal,
> Commodity . . . the plague! – that sways the world

– together with a comparison between the fictional events presented on stage and those in the world outside the theatre:

> Since sweet Commodity first tickled Eve
> 'Twas ever thus; and will be, I conceive.
> Is it not so e'en now, this latter day.

The one positive virtue Smallwood sees in the Barton *John*, albeit an ironic one, is that it makes a reader of Shakespeare's text aware of the author's careful use of his source material. In contrast with Barton's attempted clarification of the historical background, which in fact led to a confusion of focus, Shakespeare's deliberate vagueness with regard to John's and Arthur's right to the throne allows him to concentrate on what really interests him: the details of the power struggle, and the deeper underlying issue of legitimacy, moral as well as lineal. In Shakespeare's play the audience is offered a variety of claimants to the throne: 'John, Arthur, the Bastard, the Dauphin, and Prince Henry', and, in this way, invited to contemplate the 'nature of monarchy itself'. After the death of Arthur, and John's moral disqualification from the right to rule because of his role in that death, the audience is 'tempt[ed] ... to consider the Bastard, the son of Coeur-de-lion, as the inheritor of his father's position' ('Shakespeare unbalanced', p. 86). Barton's heavy-handed introduction, in the penultimate scene, of a will in the Bastard's favour, along with the substantial extension of John's role in the last two acts, unbalanced Shakespeare's delicately-achieved comparison between the morally-ascendant Bastard and the corrupt John. The Bastard's function as commentator, throughout the play, on 'the hypocritical pomposity' of the power-seekers was undercut by the fact that the characters were already 'aware of their own absurdity' (*ibid.*, p. 94).

Reviews in newspapers and periodicals focused on two central issues: were Barton's alterations theatrically effective, and had he the right to make them in the first place? Though finding the production 'enthralling', Garry O'Connor (*Plays and Players*, vol. XXI, May 1974) felt that it raised 'a great number of questions about our approach to a dead author's text', questions which could only be partially answered in the context of whether or not the end result worked in the theatre. John Barton's statement in the 1974 programme, 'In a sense any production of a play is an adaptation of the original ... a production cannot help creating as well as criticising, so turning the original text into something it is not by itself', had clearly not met with a favourable response in some quarters. The *Coventry Evening Telegraph* pointed out that *King John* was infrequently performed, and it was therefore 'irritating to find oneself responding to a director's self-indulgent conceptualising (outside the terms of reference of the text) rather than the play itself' (21 March 1974). J. C. Trewin wrote: 'We are at Stratford and we should be listening to Shakespeare' (*The Birmingham Post*, 22 March 1974). Robert Cushman in *The Observer* (24 March 1974) likened watching the production to reliving the process of constructing the piece alongside John Barton. 'We witness the enthronement of the adaptor-director, transformed as the contending princes of the play are transformed, when they assume ... the golden mask of kingship. The title acquires a double edge.' John Barber in *The Daily Telegraph* (21 March 1974) contrasted Brecht's rewriting of Shakespeare for 'an urgent political purpose' with Barton whose 'fundamental presumption . . . is that Shakespeare was a bore' who needs to be improved. For a number of reviewers, however, Shakespeare's *King John* clearly *was* something of a bore, and John Barton was to be commended for the new life he had breathed into the play. Felix Barker (*Evening News*, 21 March 1974) considered it 'small beer compared to vintage Shakespeare . . . Stratford [made] it seem almost worth the trouble.' To Michael Billington in *The Guardian* (21 March 1974), Barton's amalgamated John was 'a complex, sprawling, densely textured play that [he] found infinitely more fascinating than the published Shakespearean version'. The debate over the success of the Barton version *vis-à-vis* the original continued in 1975. J. C. Trewin asked: 'What is the excuse for a superfluous paste-up? We know that the original play works' (*Birmingham Evening Post*, 10 January 1975). Milton Shulman was of the opinion that John Barton had 'succeeded only in turning one bad play into another' (*Evening Standard*, 10 January 1975). Irving Wardle, however, applauded the further adaptation of what, the previous year, had seemed to him 'potentially the most exciting work of the season' (*The Times*, 10 January 1975), and, in the *Morning Star*, Colin Chambers noted that the production 'transforms what is usually one of the Bard's dullest pieces into a bold, Punch-and-Judy type of morality play about power politics' (11 January 1975).

In the main, even those reviewers who were unhappy about Barton's assumption of authorship found the production visually effective. The setting included sparse, grey 'traverse curtains', to facilitate scene changes, 'and emblematic props, combin[ing] simplicity and fluency' (*The Guardian*, 21 March 1974). A 'sky', studded with stars, roofed the stage and against the prevailing browns, white and black of the costumes such items as the coronation cloak and Pandulph's scarlet robes stood out boldly. Key visual moments that were commended included Lewis and Blanche sadly dancing to the sound of gunfire after the resumption of hostilities; 'little Arthur (Benedict Taylor) all in gold, sitting impassive on the ground while great powers at a table behind him discuss his fate' (B. A. Young, *Financial Times*, 21 March 1974); and Arthur's stylised fall from the walls of his prison: 'As if in a dream, he quietly treads down the steely scaffolding, pronouncing his own death with a wisdom that avoids silliness and becomes magical' (Michael Coveney, *Financial Times*, 10 January 1975).

The quality of the acting was generally praised, Emrys James's 'grinning, peremptory, jingoistic clown' of a John (*The Times*, 21 March 1974) being seen by a number of reviewers as developing into a figure of tragic dimensions in the course of the performance. Christopher Hudson in the *Evening Standard* commented favourably on the poisoning scene in Swinstead Abbey – criticised in various reviews because of its length, pretentiousness or irrelevance – for the greater three-dimensionality it gave to the character of John 'where before there was little more than a cypher' (21 March 1974). In his 1975 review, Irving Wardle argued that, despite any qualifications that might remain about the production as a whole, 'there is no question that it now offers a great protagonist'. Pandulph's striking presence and spectacular costume led to the use of some vivid descriptive phrases: a 'gargantuan ecclesiastical coal-hod, ever ready to fuel the flames of hell at the first sniff of heresy' (*Stratford-upon-Avon Herald*, 30 March 1974) being a particularly effective example. The portrayal of the Bastard (by Richard Pasco in 1974 and Ian McKellen in 1975) received a mixed response. In a generally unfavourable review of the production as a whole, J. C. Trewin praised 'Richard Pasco's magnificent Bastard' (*The Birmingham Post*, 22 March 1974), and Michael Billington (*The Guardian*, 21 March 1974) noted his progression from Tony Lumpkin to 'voice of England'. Irving Wardle, however, found Pasco too sensitive an actor to embody successfully Barton's conception of the role, and Robert Cushman pointed to 'the audible, if probably unconscious, changes of gear in Mr Pasco's delivery' (*The Observer*, 24 March 1974) that resulted from the rewriting even of the 'Commodity' speech. In 1975, Michael

Billington found that McKellen stressed the humour of the early scenes overmuch, but gained genuine moral stature as the play progressed. John Barber (*The Daily Telegraph*, 10 January, 1975), however, considered McKellen 'a jaunty but unconvincing Bastard'. Like Jeffery Dench (Pandulph), Sheila Allen as Constance was generally favourably received, though the terms in which a number of reviewers couched their responses revealed the fact that, once again, the character was seen in an unsympathetic light: 'Constance tears her hair effectively' (*The Sunday Telegraph*, 24 March 1974); 'a believably intolerable Constance' (*The Times*, 21 March 1974); 'Sheila Allen even makes the moaning Constance a figure of tragic substance' (*The Guardian*, 10 January 1975).

Whether or not the critics approved of Barton's adaptations basically depended on their attitude to Shakespeare's original play. Those who found this tedious or hopelessly incoherent generally favoured Barton's approach, while the comments of the remainder were reminiscent of Medley's view of the Colley Cibber character in Fielding's *The Historical Register*: 'as Shakespeare is already good enough for people of taste, he must be altered to the palates of those who have none; and if you will grant that, who can be properer to alter him for the worse?' Like Cibber, John Barton rewrote *King John* to make it more like a play (a more coherent and accessible play, at least) than he had found it in Shakespeare. Once again, a valid play was defined as a unified one, unity of theme being substituted for the classical unities.

Unity, of theme and political ideas, has, however, been precisely what twentieth-century critical opinion has sought for in *King John*. Commentators have looked chiefly to a concept of England, and the Bastard's function as the voice of that England, to provide the play with a coherence of perspective. Barton rejected this interpretation of the Bastard and of England. His two adaptations found their sense of unity through a view of England – and all centres and structures of power – as hopelessly corrupt. The most pervasive quality of the two Barton *King John*s was their atmosphere of fatalism. In Barton's world, everyone was tainted, even Arthur through his momentary desire to become a king. The Bastard's interpolated speech: 'I have sworn allegiance to a corrupted king / And now belike I am myself corrupt' demonstrated the fact that he, too, was sullied by the mire that surrounded him. For Barton, all action was corrupted by self-interest and politicians were distinguished only by their degree of cunning and determination to hold fast to power. The multiple coronations mocked the very notion of kingship. Building on Planché's early nineteenth-century perception that, once an actual crown is used in performance, a decision must be taken regarding the nature of that crown – and therefore of kingship itself – Barton provided a dunce's cap for John's final coronation, thus underlining John's childish folly in holding fast to the role of king, no matter what the cost.

The absurdity of clinging to power in the face of human greed and the inevitability, and finality, of death, was emphasised further, in the 1975 production, when the Bastard replaced the lost crown with one fashioned from John's will. A real crown was revealed as being as liable to destruction as a paper one, and the wishes of a dead king set at nought. Even a live one was of little consequence, for, in this version, the future King Henry was a silent, puppet-like child. When the Bastard read the final words – 'Naught shall make us rue / If England to itself do rest but true!'– it was as though such a patriotic notion had validity only within a fictionalised account of events. The reality was a bleak and disintegrating world, menaced by external forces and protected from within only by antiquated words in an outdated book.

A sense of bleakness and disintegration is characteristic also of Shakespeare's *King John*, in which the affirmative ending is preceded by a patchwork of scenes depicting victory and defeat as seemingly random, without clearly assignable causes. Barton's adaptations, therefore, were a valid response to elements which are part of the original text, though they were simplistic by comparison with the ambiguities of Shakespeare's play.

The concluding chapters of this book discuss two 1980s

productions of *King John*, both of which used Shakespeare's text, the BBC television version almost uncut, and the Warner *King John*, in its entirety. The two productions offer radically different responses to the vexed question of the play's coherence, and also to the concept of patriotism, and of England.

CHAPTER V

The BBC television
production, 1984

David Giles's television production of *King John* was recorded
in the first seven days of February 1984 as part of a BBC project
to film all Shakespeare's plays, between 1978 and 1985, with the
intention of making them available throughout the world to
audiences who might have no other access to Shakespeare's
work. Prior to this production, the BBC had filmed the eight
plays which make up the two tetralogies, David Giles directing
Richard II, the two parts of *Henry IV* and *Henry V*, and Jane
Howell the three parts of *Henry VI* and *Richard III*. Both
tetralogies, especially the Howell productions, emphasised the
continuing effects of initial acts of bloodshed from one genera-
tion to the next. Jane Howell saw the four plays she directed as
expressive of a consistent darkening of mood, 'a historical development from an age of chivalry to an age of conscienceless,
ruthless killing, a breakdown in order and ethics' (*Henry VI*,
Part 2, BBC ed., p. 18). For David Giles, a crucial element of the
tetralogy he worked on – as it would be later with *King John* –
was the contrast the plays reveal between public and private
worlds. The two parts of *Henry IV* he saw as more realistic and
private than *Richard II*. In the *Henry IV* plays, he noted, 'it all
happens in rooms: in the Boar's Head, in Warkworth Castle,
and often the scenes are just duologues' (*Henry IV*, Part 1, BBC
ed., p. 20). *Henry V*, by contrast, was the most stylised of the

[84]

four plays because of its use of a chorus, and its concentration on the public image of Henry – an image which, in Giles's view, Henry consciously adopted. The Chorus and the public face of Henry presented the official, idealised picture of the king, but occasionally the anxieties of the private man showed through, for example in his prayer before battle when he was assailed by the fear that his father's guilt in Richard's murder might be laid to his charge also and lead to his defeat. This focus on kingship as a public role is a further element which, along with the contrast between public and private scenes, links the Giles tetralogy with *King John*.

Stylisation of *King John*

David Giles saw *King John* as dividing stylistically into three parts: Act I (itself separable into two sections very dissimilar in style – the formal, public scene which opens the play, and then the quite different, 'almost comedy scene between the Bastard and his brother and the Bastard and Lady Faulconbridge and John's judgement, like the judgement of Solomon, about whom the Faulconbridge land belongs to'); the 'emblematic' Acts II and III in which 'virtually everything happens in public'; and the 'more realistic' final two acts with their greater number of duologues (BBC ed., pp. 21 and 22). Clearly if Acts II and III were to be stylised, it would be difficult to use fully realistic sets for the remainder of the play. Some differentiation needed to be made, however, between scenes based on rhetoric intended for public consumption, and others in which small groups of individuals grappled to come to an accommodation with confusing and turbulent events. Designer Chris Pemsel's solution was to use for Acts II and III 'a huge sky cloth which [was] not only a brilliant blue but [was] decorated by golden fleur-de-lis, as though the whole action of the play were taking place beneath a heraldic canopy' (*ibid.*, p. 22). Angiers was represented by a pale-blue tower and battlements resembling cardboard cut-outs, and the French and English positions by pretty, toy-like tents and fluttering pennants. The setting for Act I was more substantial, but, again, the emphasis was on decorative effect. Walls, pillars and arches were painted, chiefly with lozenge and zigzag patterns, the preponderant colours being grey, black, white and dark red. The king's throne was on a red dais. This setting was used again for IV.ii and V.i. The third scene of Act IV (Arthur's leap from his prison wall, and his subsequent discovery by the English lords), was played in a childlike setting similar to the cardboard cut-out that had represented Angiers. Of the remaining scenes, IV.i (the threatened blinding of Arthur) had the most realistic setting, a room divided by a heavy curtain which hid the glowing coals and instruments of torture from view until they were needed. To provide a link with Act I and signify the return to England, the arch and passage-way seen at the back of the set were ornamented once again with similar patterns and colours. With the exception of the penultimate scene, where the required atmosphere was established through dim lighting, all the later scenes were played against picturesque representations of frequently stormy-looking skies, a device which was valuable both for its atmospheric effect and for the degree of unity it added to the episodic and fragmented final section of the play.

The toy-town quality of the setting was particularly effective in Act II, where it underlined the childish attitudinising of the various characters, each of whom had a doll-like quality. When the Citizen of Angiers loomed above the pretty little battlements, he lent a sense of scale to the wrangling of the diminutive kings. Shakespeare's basic cast in Act II was augmented by a number of spear bearers, or, more correctly, banner and shield bearers, representing the English and French forces. They were mostly static, and, on the small screen, with its lack of depth, they created a frieze-like effect. As the key characters moved to positions of greater prominence to state their various cases, it was as if each figure became temporarily detached from the frieze, an important result of this being an enhanced focus on the publicly perceived role of each character, king, warrior queen, injured mother, rather than on a character's individual qualities.

Costumes emphasised both the public role and the toy-like attributes of the characters. King Philip of France in a robe composed of delicate and exotic layers of blue fabrics, with sleeves which appeared to be made from the thinnest possible wafers of gold tissue, had a puppet-like stillness which afforded only occasional glimpses of the human being that inhabited the splendour. John wore a gold cloak and red robe with a cluster of three white flowers with stalk and leaves on sleeves and bodice (probably a rose, but, just possibly, representative of broom – *planta genesta* – an emblem of John's grandfather, Geoffrey of Anjou, and source of the name Plantagenet). Eleanor, likened by Peter Kemp in a review in the *Times Literary Supplement* (7 December 1984) to 'a glittery-eyed, leather-skinned old reptile', was resplendent in shiny gold, black and silvery grey. She stood ramrod straight, an indomitable warrior queen. Beside her, the more youthful Constance was soft and rounded in a close-fitting, dove-grey dress with, on her head, a gossamer-thin veil, surmounted by a fairy-tale crown. The costumes of all the court characters had a fairy-tale quality. Throughout, this was a production that was both visually exquisite and almost excessively tidy. With the exception of the Bastard, whose hair did at least occasionally look a little ruffled, and Peter of Pomfret, whose brief appearance afforded a glimpse of a less manicured world, all the characters, even messengers arriving hotfoot from scenes of devastation, were impeccably attired and had perfectly coiffured hair.

Though the stylised costumes and setting were effective in Act II, where they reduced the bombast of the characters to the posturings of animated dolls, the cardboard cut-out battlements worked less well for Arthur's death leap in IV.iii. Act II is basically satiric, and the pretty costumes and pastel shades of the set helped to make this point when seen in contrast with adult actors. Arthur's death, however, is tragic, and placing a round-faced boy actor within the toy-world had the effect of completely destroying any sense of the credibility of his death. No attempt was made through a lighting change to lessen the artificiality of the setting. Only the initial movement of the jump was shown, as the camera immediately cut away from the boy, but, when he came into shot again, he was carefully and tidily positioned at the base of the tower, a neat trickle of blood from one nostril the only indication that he was on the point of death. One had to take on trust the lords' subsequent distress when they found the body, because nothing that had been shown warranted this.

Interpretation of the Bastard and John

In addition to the big public scenes in *King John*, which it would be difficult to play realistically on television, the Bastard's direct addresses to the audience puncture further the possibility of a realistic overall approach to the play. Perhaps unsurprisingly, given the one-to-one intimacy television establishes with the viewer, these were the speeches that came over best. With the exception of a few lines of Hubert's in IV.i, the Bastard was the only character who spoke directly to camera, and he therefore became very clearly the viewer's guide to an understanding of the play's events. George Costigan's Bastard was an interesting interpretation in that it worked extremely well within the restrained televisual style of performance, yet, at the same time, his characterisation, like Leonard Rossiter's John, was essentially a conventional one. Inconsistent and childish, Rossiter's portrayal lacked the 'kingly' qualities of Michael Hordern's or Robert Harris's characterisation, but it was recognisably within a tradition which stretches back to Macready's depiction which Leigh Hunt described as being 'like the real historical King John, the vacillating, weak, wilful monarch'. Unfortunately, however, Rossiter's John lacked a strong inner dynamic. He was himself aware in rehearsals of the problems he was having with the role, especially the notorious difficulty of finding a through line of motivation for John's actions. The result was a performance which Peter Kemp described as 'over-mannered' and, in the main, not 'very compelling', though his playing of the final scene was distinctive and effective.

George Costigan's portrayal of the Bastard was both assured

and reflective of the frequently expressed critical view that this is the play's central character. Costigan played the Bastard as an intelligent, likeable man, a little cocky to begin with but compassionate and caring, particularly towards his mother whom he treated with great tenderness, and Eleanor for whom it was obvious that he had conceived an immediate, and clearly reciprocated, affection and respect. His counterpart in the nineteenth century would therefore be Charles Kemble, of whom Mrs Cowden Clarke wrote that 'in the scene with his mother . . . his manly tenderness, his filial coaxing way of speaking and putting his arm around her as he thanks her for having made Richard Coeur de Lion his father, was something to be grateful for having witnessed'.

Like his performance, the costumes Costigan wore allied this interpretation with the conventional view that the Bastard is the play's hero and the 'voice of England'. His rise in social status was reflected in his rich clothes from Act II onwards, his simple woollen tunic of Act I being replaced by a magnificently embroidered version in gold, black and grey – Eleanor's colours. The two garments were linked, however, by the presence on each of them of a thick, dark, diagonal stripe running from the top right-hand corner of the neck (from the perspective of the wearer), to the bottom left. The reference point for this device, which is an echo of Smith's costume design for the Faulconbridge family in the Macready *John*, was the armorial bearing on the Bastard's shield, a single lion rampant, his father's emblem, on a bend (a diagonal stripe on a shield from the top right corner to the left of the base). Around his neck, Costigan wore a large circular collar, with a patterning suggestive of the sun's rays, or conceivably a lion's mane, either design signifying heroic status.

Constance and Blanche

Prior to her 'mad' scene in III.iv, Claire Bloom's costume as Constance emphasised the actress's naturally feminine appearance. Though she was vigorously determined in the passages in which Constance defends her son, her delicate robes and crown made her the visual antithesis of the ferocious and sardonic Eleanor of Mary Morris. Blanche, played by Janet Maw, seemed, however, a younger version of Constance. Dressed from her first entrance in white (potential bride, sacrifice, or both?) Blanche too wore on her head a crown of exquisite filigree work. This questioning of the significance of the choice of white for Blanche's costume is apposite because, in its high-lighting of the powerlessness of Blanche and Constance, the BBC *King John* was more radical than it was in its depiction of the Bastard and John. In III.i, for example, first Blanche, and then Constance kneel to plead with Lewis, the Dauphin. Blanche, who has just become Lewis's wife, begs him to remain true to his recent alliance with her uncle, John, whereas Constance urges him to return to his earlier loyalty and fight on her son's behalf. David Giles's production stressed the women's shared helplessness rather than their opposing claims. As they knelt in turn to Lewis to try to persuade him of the justice of their points of view, each, in her pale-coloured robes, fluttering veil, and with a crown seemingly of spun-sugar on her head, seemed virtually a mirror-image of the other. In one telling shot, the only part of Lewis visible on screen was his ermine sleeve, but this was sufficient to establish his authority and power – a synecdoche of greatness. By contrast, the two women, shown from the waist upwards, hands pleadingly stretched towards the princely sleeve, were powerless. Their very similarity emphasised the lack of worth that would be accorded to their individual claims.

Blanche's role is a small one. She disappears from the play at the end of III.i, after her abortive attempt to persuade her husband to side with John, and before the final exit of Eleanor and Constance. In the eighteenth and nineteenth centuries Blanche's already sparse lines were drastically cut, and it has generally been a thankless part in the twentieth century, review-ers noting chiefly the charming qualities of the actress. The TV Blanche *was* pretty and charming, but she also had a certain astuteness, an air, for example, as she surveyed the two kings who congratulated her on her marriage to Lewis, of trying to work out her own precise significance in the affair. 'The sun's o'ercast with blood' speech at the end of III.i. she began as the various factions swirled round her preparing themselves for the coming battle. As she spoke the following lines, the combatants formed themselves into opposed groups leaving her in the centre.

> Husband, I cannot pray that thou mayst win;
> Uncle, I needs must pray that thou mayst lose;
> Father, I may not wish the fortune thine;
> Grandam, I will not wish thy wishes thrive.
> Whoever wins, on that side shall I lose:
> Assurèd loss, before the match be play'd (331–6)

Her costume was still that of a fairy-tale princess, but her words and her positioning defined her helplessness.

In a variety of ways Claire Bloom's performance offered a reappraisal of the character of Constance. The small-scale, intimate nature of television inevitably led to a quieter, more restrained interpretation than is usual in the theatre, and reduced the likelihood of Constance appearing to be a 'wailing woman'. In addition, Claire Bloom challenged the conventional view of the character by portraying Constance as eminently sane and reasonable. When she sat on the ground in III.i, on the lines 'Here I and sorrows sit / Here is my throne, bid kings come bow to it', she did so in a controlled and deliberate manner, calmly certain of victory. Bloom did 'not regard the final "so-called mad scene" as being in fact a mad scene.' Instead, she saw Constance as 'a woman of tremendous intellect', who uses words with a dexterity matched only by Pandulph. 'No woman in Shakespeare has such complex language . . . But it's difficult for a reason. In that so-called mad scene her arguments are so modern, so anti-clerical and so clever!' (BBC ed., p. 28). The hallmark of Claire Bloom's performance was its rationality. When, on Pandulph's accusation that she 'utter[ed] madness and not sorrow', she sat on the other side from him of a small wooden table, and calmly and logically defended her sanity, the fact that she sat in a position equal to Pandulph added to the reasonableness of her words. It was only on her final lines that she broke down. Traditionally, actresses have rent their hair, or torn off a head-dress of some kind on the words 'I will not keep this form upon my head', but for Claire Bloom the 'form' Constance refers to was the 'terrible order and control she's had all these years'. Her Constance found it 'an *effort* . . . to go mad' (*ibid.*), and it was only on her exit lines that she suggested a mind in process of becoming unhinged.

The placing of the interval

The decision to take the sole interval at the end of Act II was an unusual one, as this is a very early point in the action. More usually, if there is only one interval, this is taken after III.iii (the scene in which Hubert agrees to Arthur's death), as, for example, it was in Douglas Seale's 1957 production, or at the end of Act III, as was the case in Deborah Warner's RSC production which is discussed in the next chapter. This latter choice has an obvious logic in that Act III concludes the action in France, and it means that the second half begins with IV.i, the scene which marks the move to a focus on individual responses to public events. Part One of the BBC *King John* was composed of two acts, the first set in England, the second in France, each rounded off by the Bastard. He was the weather-vane that pointed the viewer towards changes in the play's moral climate. In Act I, after gleefully anatomising the 'worshipful society' of which he was now part, he used his complicity with the camera to woo the viewer to an acceptance of his own right to learn from the spirit of the times, and to 'deliver / Sweet, sweet, sweet poison for the age's tooth'. His rueful look to camera after asserting his determination to behave in future in a self-interested way was clearly indicative of his realisation of the viewer's possible disapproval, but it revealed also the expectation that s/he would share his delight in this new world. A sequence of action in the 'Commodity' speech which ends Act II provided a link with this moment in the Act I soliloquy. After his lengthy and impassioned condemnation of Commodity, Costigan suddenly began to laugh at the irony of his distaste now for the very

[92]

form of behaviour he had wished to ape. His final tribute to Commodity, despite his understanding of its essentially corrupt nature – 'Gain, be my lord, for I will worship thee' – ended Part One with a view of a world in which even the possession of integrity seemed little defence against the prevailing climate of self-interest.

Part Two began with Constance's 'Gone to be married?' speech, but Claire Bloom's restrained style of performance meant that there was no problem for the viewer in returning to the action at this point. In fact, Constance's question was helpful in refocusing attention on a crucial element of the plot. A particular gain from playing Act IV immediately after Act III was that Pandulph's political seduction of Lewis the Dauphin was juxtaposed with Hubert's decision to save Arthur's life. In each of these two duologues an older man holds power over someone many years his junior. In III.iv the white-clad Pandulph (Richard Wordsworth), whose costume when he first appeared in III.i suggested saintliness, and the Dauphin (Jonathan Coy), in chain-mail decorated with fleur-de-lis, sat one each side of the table outside the French tent. As in the scene with Constance, their similar positioning seemed to confer equality of status. In reality, however, the honours lay with Cardinal Pandulph, who, with a dexterity so smooth and silken as to be barely recognisable as the politicking it in fact was, spun the Dauphin, a cautious but not quite sufficiently astute fly, into his web. Lewis's gradual enmeshment was revealed by his changing facial expressions. At first he was dismissive of the Cardinal's arguments, but, on the brief, pregnant pause after 'which shall directly lead / Thy foot to England's throne' (129–30), he quickly looked up from the goblet of wine he held in his hand, his attention finally caught, even if he was as yet uncertain whether or not to fall in with Pandulph's plans. When the Dauphin suggested that John might, after all, not harm Arthur, Richard Wordsworth's slight hesitation before the word 'gone' in the following passage was an object lesson in the art of political euphemism.

O, sir, when he shall hear of your approach,
If that young Arthur be not gone already,
Even at that news he dies. (162–4)

His promise that a handful of French soldiers would be sufficient to draw ten thousand of the English to their side, just as 'a
little snow, tumbled about / Anon becomes a mountain' (176–7),
signalled the Dauphin's little smile of agreement. The latter's
vehemently whispered 'Strong reasons make strong actions'
(182) was fully revelatory of the degree of understanding he had
reached in the workings of Commodity (even if he hadn't yet
grasped his own manipulation in Commodity's name). In the
background chanting monks drew a veil of sanctity over the
grubby dealings of the apprentice in the art of self-interest and
his mentor.

The effectiveness of IV.i was limited by the difficulty the
young Luc Owen had with Shakespeare's formalised language.
Despite a general twentieth-century perception of this scene as
hopelessly sentimental, boy actors *have* been praised in the role
of Arthur, though often in conjunction with comments on their
inability to speak the verse properly. Approximately forty of
Arthur's lines were cut in the television version, and, as few
lines were omitted from the text as a whole, this presumably
reflects the difficulty Luc Owen had in speaking the words so
that a complicated thought-process was made clear to the very
end of each line and speech. Visually, he was an effective
Arthur. Small, innocent-looking, in a simple, pale-coloured tunic reflective of his lowly victim status, he formed a strong
contrast with Pandulph in the previous scene, an image of true
goodness against the Cardinal's false holiness. Arthur's seeming
helplessness turns out to be his best form of defence, as its
effect is to disarm Hubert. As a result of the Hubert/Arthur
scene being placed immediately after that between Pandulph
and Lewis, a lesson in Commodity became followed by an
exposition of the power of innocence. The phoney saint who
showed his pupil 'the bias of the world' was succeeded by a
child who taught the dark, menacing Hubert, excellently played
by John Thaw, a very different lesson, a lesson, moreover,

fundamental to an understanding of the shape of the final section of the play.

The Bastard *vis-à-vis* the Dauphin

The Bastard, the character who identifies Commodity as the force that sways the world from its true course, is, with Hubert, the chief resister of Commodity's lure. Both characters, after seemingly committing themselves to a course of action governed by self-interest, make positive decisions to place a higher good above that of self. The Bastard's opposite number in the television production was very definitely the Dauphin, who became increasingly skilled in the art of Commodity as the Bastard neglected opportunities to base his actions on the pursuit of gain. After his encounter with Pandulph, Lewis is not seen again until V.ii. In the television version, this scene (set in the Dauphin's camp at St Edmundsbury) was played, similarly to III.iv, around a wooden table in front of a tent, though with the difference that the blue backcloth ornamented with fleur-de-lis was replaced by a representation of a cloud-wracked sky. Lewis's political expertise at this point was revealed by his response to Lord Salisbury's grief at his enforced participation in the future slaughter of his countrymen now that he had joined the French side in the war. As Salisbury openly wept, Lewis, through small facial movements, registered his contempt to the Count Melun who sat beside him. When he stood, however, and praised Salisbury's nobility, his face was controlled, his words, though largely meaningless in their hyperbole, slickly delivered. The true measure of his political ability came with the entrance of Pandulph bringing news of John's reconciliation with Rome and the consequent need for the French to cease hostilities against him. Jonathan Coy's playing of the Dauphin's mounting anger at Pandulph's attempt to treat him once again as a pawn in the Church's power game showed the distance he had travelled since the last meeting between the two men. His stance towards Pandulph and the Bastard in the latter part of the scene, back negligently turned away, signalled his

[95]

assurance and his determination to take note of neither of them.

The Dauphin's final appearance in the play is also the occasion of the news of the end of the French hopes of victory. The television production began the scene with a sense of quiet confidence. Against a dark night sky, relieved by the light of a flambeau, the Dauphin had just taken off his crown – presumably to rest from the labours of the day now that success seemed within his grasp – when a black-robed messenger came silently into view. The news of the Count Melun's death was delivered publicly, but the grim tidings of the defection of the English lords and the French losses on Goodwin Sands were spoken softly and furtively, for the Dauphin's ear alone. Despite his shocked grasp of the defeat that now stared him in the face, the Dauphin's continued mastery of his public role was abundantly evident in his confident-seeming promise to those around him: 'The day shall not be up so soon as I / To try the fair adventure of to-morrow' (V.v.21–2). His helpless look towards the Messenger at the end of this speech, however, was eloquent of his loss of control over future happenings. His grasp of the mechanics of Commodity was finally revealed to be of little value to him, because he had been beaten by the arbitrariness of events.

The Bastard's words, 'Gain, be my lord, for I will worship thee' (II.i.598), which ended Part One in the television version, never in fact seem to form a particularly strong motivation for his actions – though they could serve as the motto for many of the other characters – and the discovery of the dead body of Prince Arthur in IV.iii strengthens his fidelity to the English cause. For the actor George Costigan the Bastard's love of England was the character's central motivating force. Costigan saw John as 'a terrible king, [with] no sense of loyalty or vision', and he decided that the Bastard 'backs up . . . the *concept* of royalty, the throne, rather than the man' (BBC ed., p. 25). At the end of V.i he reacted to Leonard Rossiter's childish relief at the papal legate's manoeuvrings on his behalf with a frenzied attempt to rouse John to some semblance of greatness, which caused the terrified king to cower back into the corner of his throne. On his next entrance, in the Dauphin's camp, the Bastard himself provided the image of England that he had so signally failed to elicit from the king. Draped in his father's lion's skin that he had won from the archduke of Austria, he was every inch the hero John so manifestly was not.

The use of the lion's skin to signify heroism was, like the diagonal stripe on his costume and Costigan's general approach to the character, a link with the traditional concept of the Bastard. The substitution, in the nineteenth century, of a lion's skin for Austria's head in III.ii was noted in Chapter II. In the eighteenth century, Francis Gentleman put forward the suggestion that 'the lion's skin, as a trophy of honour worn by his father, should be worn by the Bastard through the remainder of the play' (Sprague, *Shakespeare and the Actors*, p. 111). Only at the point in the play when he spoke on John's behalf, however, did George Costigan as the Bastard put on the emblem of the dead king, his father, and so represent in his own person the *concept* of royalty'.

Role, kinship, and the final scene

In the production as a whole, costume served to enhance the public roles of the characters. The fact that virtually the entire cast wore crowns or fillets of precious metals on their heads pointed to the royal or noble status of almost all the figures in the play, and bought into focus the English lords' dismissal of Hubert as a commoner – plus the true nobility of his actions. In Blanche's case, her white dress, in addition to her crown, revealed her to be both royal and virgin, a valuable bargaining counter in the eventual deal between France and England. Pandulph's white garments functioned as a carapace, a mask of sanctity which initially hid his mastery of political manoeuvre. In III.iv Constance's putting off of her veil and crown and assumption of a rough cloak over her earlier costume effectively freed her from the trappings that had held her within her previous role. The image she presented in her final scene was ambiguous. On the one hand, her long, loose hair was suggestive of a traditional presentation of a madwoman; on the other, her controlled speech stressed her rationality. Within the character of Constance in this scene, therefore, the private individual was at odds with the publicly perceived role. It was both ironic and understandable that Philip and Pandulph, two master-manipulators of the public image, should take note of only the conventional aspects of madness she presented and not the signs that contradicted the role of madwoman. As in David Giles's production of *Henry V*, the relationship between individual and role was an important element in *King John*. Constance attempted to escape from the imposed role of madwoman. The Dauphin assumed a politically effective public face, and then displayed it to the end, revealing only through tiny changes of expression, directed towards those in his confidence, the private individual behind the role. Leonard Rossiter's John was always *prescribed* by his role as king. Even in death he was a monarch rather than a man, a point which will be considered further in the discussion of the final scene.

The Bastard defines for himself a role the Dauphin will later adopt, that of apprentice to Commodity, but then shows little interest in playing it. Briefly, he tries out a self-serving public image, but then chooses to follow the dictates of a higher good. Nowhere was his spontaneity and humanity, as opposed to the status-ridden actions of those around him, more evident than in his relationship with his mother and grandmother, whom he kissed on the mouth in moments of strong emotion, and treated always with tenderness and respect. When, at the end of Act I, he firmly, yet gently, impelled his mother to go with him to meet his 'kin', his loving pride in the woman he would introduce to Eleanor and John was obvious. With Eleanor he maintained an affectionate raillery that showed his deep admiration as well as his love for his kinswoman.

The importance of kinship and the link between individual and role were structuring elements of the final scene of the television *King John*. In the orchard of Swinstead Abbey, represented by a cloth of a dawn sky and by leafless trees veiled in thin mist, Prince Henry, Salisbury and Bigot entered slowly to the sound of a clock striking and monks chanting. In features and stature Rusty Livingstone, as Henry, looked remarkably like an older edition of Arthur. Like Luc Owen, he wore a short tunic, but, in his case, of a soft green colour, suggestive, in opposition to the wintry trees, of spring and a possibly better future state of affairs. When the lords knelt to him at the end of the play in affirmation of his right to be England's king, his resemblance to Arthur partly blotted out the misery of his cousin's death. One young claimant to the English throne had died tragically and needlessly, but another and similar heir had appeared unexpectedly, almost magically, to offer hope of a transformation after the sterile disorder of John's reign. This ending, therefore, was in marked contrast to the ending of Barton's *King John*, particularly in 1975, when the same actor was used in the roles of both Arthur and Henry, so reinforcing the overall pessimism of the production.

Leonard Rossiter, as King John, sat in the chair in which he had been carried into the orchard wearing a stained and decaying nightgown, but with hair and beard neatly groomed, his body still and stiff as a doll, his rasping voice that of an automaton. As he spoke his last words, 'all this thou seest is but a clod / And module of confounded royalty', the validity of this observation was emphasised by his head slowly and mechanically swivelling first to one side, then to the other, and by the index finger which he raised to draw attention to what he was saying. He became a clockwork-toy king, and his machinery finally ran down and stopped, the actual moment of death signified by only the tiniest of head movements. The blankness of his face in death, though eerie, seemed hardly distinguishable from the fixed mask of kingship he had exhibited in the final moments of life.

Though the production ended with a general exodus, following the chanting monks who carried John's body back to the Abbey, the Bastard's concluding speech, filmed in close-up, was the true climax of the piece. After expressing grief at John's death, the Bastard had quickly turned his attention to the safety of the nation, urging the lords to join him in his mission of expelling the French forces from the land. As he learned, belatedly, of the almost-completed peace treaty, he was momentarily disconcerted, but then took a different kind of control of the situation, offering a lead to the lords in his immediate homage to Henry. As he spoke the final tribute to England, the camera focused on his head and shoulders, the beautiful circular collar he wore, with its pattern of sun's rays or lion's mane, enhancing his heroic status. In the character of the Bastard, who understood the workings of Commodity but whose actions were those of a man of integrity, the interconnection between individual and role found a new formulation. Whereas John was, by the end, nothing but the husk of a king because the inner man had always, at best, been thin and ghostly, the Bastard's humanity gave life and substance to the conventional role of hero. The championship of Prince Henry by the man who had always behaved lovingly to his womenfolk, and showed deep grief at the death of one young cousin, offered to another the possibility of a successful reign and, to England, the chance of security and peace.

With the exception of its portrayal of Constance and, in some respects, of Blanche, the television *King John* was fundamentally a conservative interpretation. Its chief values lay in its demonstration of the continuing effectiveness of such an interpretation in performance, and the way in which it made generally available a relatively unknown Shakespearean play. It had the further advantage of offering valuable insights into the relationship in the play between individual and role. Deborah Warner's 1988/89 RSC production, however, attempted to begin from scratch, to jettison preconceptions regarding how the play works, or fails to work, and to examine more fully also *King John*'s relevance to the late twentieth-century world.

Patrick Stewart as King John in Buzz Goodbody's 1970 Theatre-go-round production. Photo: Joe Cocks Studio

Emry James as King John in John Barton's adaptation of the play.
Photo: Joe Cocks Studio

Benedict Taylor as Prince Arthur in the Barton *King John*.
Photo: Joe Cocks Studio

Emry James (John) and Jeffery Dench (Pandulph) in the Barton *King John*.
Photo: Joe Cocks Studio

facing
Sue Blane's set for Deborah Warner's production of *King John*.
Photo: Joe Cocks Studio

Nicholas Woodeson as John in Act II of the Deborah Warner production.
Photo: Joe Cocks Studio

Susan Engel as Constance in Act III, scene iv (Deborah Warner production). Photo: Joe Cocks Studio

'The joining of hands' (Act V, scene ii) in the Warner *King John*.
From left to right: Lewis, the Dauphin, Ralph Fiennes; Lord Bigot, Darryl
Forbes-Dawson; Earl of Pembroke, Richard Bremmer; Earl of Salisbury,
Edward Harbour. Photo: Joe Cocks Studio

CHAPTER VI

Deborah Warner's production: Stratford-upon-Avon, 1988 and London,1989

On 4 May 1988, Deborah Warner's production of *King John* opened at The Other Place in Stratford. Sadly the 'corrugated iron hut' (Chambers, *Other Spaces*, p. 7), which once constituted the RSC's alternative Stratford venue, no longer exists. As a theatre it certainly had drawbacks. It tended to be hot and stuffy in the summer, cold and initially unwelcoming in winter, and the dressing-rooms and other facilities for the company were woefully inadequate; but, and it is a large but, it was a wonderful place in which to see and hear a piece of theatre. Its intimacy and simplicity meant that nothing distracted: all concentration was focused on the playing space. There is now a new Other Place which is an excellent theatre, but for Warner's *King John*, characterised as it was above all by two fundamental qualities, roughness and clarity, the sparse, makeshift nature of the old building was ideal.

Roughness and clarity were essential elements of Deborah Warner's approach, which she defined in interview as 'wild, searching', and 'deliberately raw, big-brush-stroke'. From the outset, this was intentionally 'an experimental production . . . an attempt to find out what *John* was' Setting aside established wisdom as to *King John*'s strengths and weaknesses, she and the company explored the text in rehearsals in order to come to a fresh understanding of the nature of the play Shakespeare had written. She started without preconceived ideas with regard to moves, and, instead, worked to create conditions in which the actors were encouraged, enabled, constrained to explore the relationship between themselves, the text and the performance space, and to use this as a means of blocking the play. Approximately the first fortnight of rehearsals was spent in a communal exploration of the text, using in the main two methods: frequent readings of the play in which the actors were allotted parts other than the ones in which they had been cast, and translation of Shakespeare's words into the actors' own. The chief value of the first method for the actors was that they were able to experience the text as a group, rather than from the vantage-point of one, as yet only very partially comprehended, character, and for the director that she was exposed constantly to the play, and particularly to varied readings of it, at a time when her ideas as to its form and meaning were still very much in a state of flux. Putting the text into their own words meant that the whole company had to grapple with what Shakespeare's language means at every moment of the action. From about the beginning of the third week, the actors were working with Shakespeare's words and on the characters they were actually playing, exploring their own and the text's relationship to the space in which they would perform, a space described by Susan Engel, who played Constance, as having the qualities of both a tennis-court and a bullring.

The eventual production that Deborah Warner and the company devised was fast and furious, with characters hurtling on and off the playing space. As Virginia Mason Vaughan notes in 'Between tetralogies' (p. 408), *King John* begins in *medias res*. 'Now say, Chatillon, what would France with us?' John peremptorily enquires, and, on his rejection of the French demands, what speedily follows is, in John's own words, 'war for war and blood for blood / Controlment for controlment'. The course of events, once set in motion, swiftly takes on its own unstoppable logic: the claims and counterclaims, 'Controlment for controlment', of the first half being succeeded in the second part of the play by catastrophic public and private events, culminating in the spectacle of John burnt up by a poison which corrodes him from within, as England is threatened by destruction from both foreign invasion and internal revolt.

Despite the production's roughness and sense of anarchy, it was tightly controlled, and the visual effect one of great simplicity. The old Other Place was a small, roughly square-shaped box, with a central performance area. The seating was located in a thin strip round the periphery, sometimes on three sides, sometimes on four. There were also a number of seats on an upper level. For *King John* the audience were seated on three sides of the acting area. The setting was sparse (see illustrations): a timbered floor, a few serviceable wooden chairs, and a host of ladders, which were used variously to create the siege of Angiers, a table around which the acrimonious discussion following John's second coronation took place, and the battlements from which Arthur jumped. Three sequences of action – the section in III.iii where John sounds out Hubert regarding the projected murder of Arthur, the beginning of V.i (Pandulph's returning of the crown to John), and Arthur's death-leap (IV.iii) – were played on the upper level. The musicians were also seated on this level, and Hubert took up his position there in II.i. The remaining action was all played on the lower level. There were few props, and the chairs were used only in the scene after the coronation, and in IV.i, the blinding of Arthur. The text was performed uncut, a decision which Robert Smallwood suggested might well have been 'an all-time first' ('Shakespeare at Stratford', p. 92)

In line with the simplicity and improvised nature of the setting, the costumes gave the impression of having been rapidly assembled from readily available sources, an aspect which was noted by a number of reviewers. Charles Osborne, in *The Daily Telegraph* (30 May 1988), for example, commented that 'some of the characters . . . look as if they have been dressed in a hurry by Oxfam', and Michael Ratcliffe (*The Observer*, 15 May 1988) wrote: 'The appearance is timeless-modern, the clothes spattered and well used, greatcoats thrown hastily over civilian trousers and City shirts as though the wearers had been surprised by sudden civil war.' Nicholas de Jongh in *The Guardian* thought that the costumes reflected an interpretation of 'the Kings of England and France and their noble entourages' which reduced the grand wars to 'no more than games and pageants' and the characters to 'a cross between perpetual adolescents and amateur actors caught up in village hall theatricals' (4 May 1989). At the siege of Angiers, Austria wore what appeared to be an entire lion's skin, plus the head, while the Bastard had a banner of the cross of St George casually draped round him, and John was dressed like Tweedledum in a helmet the size of a coal-scuttle. His crown was chained to his waist and he had a sword as big as himself in his hand. The performance style of the big public speeches was in the same satirical vein, pointing up the distinction between public posturing and private self-interest. In Deborah Warner's words, the characters had to seen to 'be wearing their hearts bleeding on their sleeves', so that the audience would realise 'what was underneath the speeches and weep with laughter'. Accompanying the battle scenes there was live, circus-style music which further debunked the attitudinising of the various claimants to the crown. Two quotations, from reviews of the production after it transferred to The Pit in London, capture its sharply-focused, sardonic quality: 'English history as seen through the eyes of George Grosz' (Irving Wardle, *The Times*, 4 May 1989), and the headline for the review in *The Guardian* of the same date, 'A strip-cartoon Shakespeare' (Nicholas de Jongh).

Opinion among reviewers was divided with regard to the value of Deborah Warner's approach. For some, it was simplistic, a limited perspective on the play's complexity. The majority response, however, was favourable. Michael Billington, for example, in *The Guardian*, (12 May 1988, 'Ms Warner's real talent is for getting to the heart of a play by the most direct route'), praised the production's lucidity, while 'another spare, muscular and scrupulously intelligent production from that most exciting and intelligent of Shakespearian story-tellers – Deborah Warner' was Lyn Gardner's verdict in *City Limits* (2 June 1988). Paul Taylor's comment in *The Independent* (12 May

1988), 'It has the distinctive look she has created of still having one foot in the rehearsal room', captured the provisional, experimental nature of the production.

Controlment for controlment

Throughout the rehearsal process, a crucial factor governing where the characters moved on the playing area was which of them controlled a particular sequence of action. Through a collective search, the company elucidated the play's strands of debate, the shape of the text dictating the blocking, with the result that the visual patterning revealed the constant shifts in the power balance. The various contenders in the power battles come together in II.i and III.i. It is these scenes that must clearly establish the checks and counterchecks to the characters' ambitions. This is also the part of the play which must clarify the production's attitude to power and those who seek to wield it. This section therefore discusses in detail the Warner production's staging of II.i and III.i, and its interpretation of the play's depiction of the mechanics of power.

The lights dimmed after the first act, and a central spotlight then revealed Austria, with a lion's skin, complete with head, draped over his greatcoat. His solitary presence briefly echoed the opening sequence of Act I in which Chatillon, the French ambassador, had slowly paced to and fro across the stage as he waited for John to enter and respond to King Philip's demands. Unlike Chatillon, however, Austria was alone on stage only momentarily, as, almost immediately, to the sound of wild whooping and yelling, actors carrying ladders ran, one after the other, at full tilt, past him and speedily erected a barricade of ladders against the back wall of the playing space, thus creating the besieged town of Angiers. Lively circus music accompanied and accentuated the sound and action, pointing up both the ludicrousness of Austria's 'martial' costume and the theatricality of the combatants' attitude to battle. As the fast-paced drumming built to a climax, Philip, Lewis, Constance, Arthur and the Count Melun entered downstage, walked rapidly over a floor criss-crossed with the shadows of ladders and, on a final drum-beat, turned sharply to face Austria who now stood downstage centre. (Positions on the stage are from the viewpoint of those members of the audience sitting with their backs to the entrance to The Other Place.) At the same moment, the lighting swiftly changed to a bright, open state which mercilessly exposed the pomposity and self-interested natures of Austria and the French King. The fact that Arthur's speech of welcome to Austria was carefully stage-managed was evident from the way in which Philip indicated to the young prince the exact moment when he should take centre stage and by the precisely modulated round of applause with which Arthur's words were greeted. Austria's exaggerated posturings were exemplified by an absurdly elaborate ritual of blowing a kiss to Arthur as a seal of his vow to fight on the prince's behalf. The satirical 'strip-cartoon' approach to the portrayal of the characters continued with the entrance of John with his outsize helmet and sword and the Bastard wearing his St-George's-cross banner, and in the presentation of Hubert, particularly when he watched the first (offstage) battle between the two armies, from the spotlit balcony while munching on a very French-looking sausage.

Alongside the satirical presentation, however, there went a very clear delineation of the changing fortunes in the battle for power. When John entered with his huge sword over his shoulder, he stood downstage centre, thus balancing his opponent, the French King, who was upstage centre. The central area was empty, but, upon his accusation that John had 'Outfacèd infant state, and done a rape / Upon the maiden virtue of the crown' (97–8), Philip gestured to Arthur – the virgin prince who had been ravished from his rightful position – to come to centre stage, while he went on to cite Arthur's resemblance to his father, John's elder brother Geoffrey, as proof of the boy's legitimacy and right to the English crown. Arthur's central position on stage demonstrated his crucial importance in the fight for the crown, but his small, powerless, almost silent figure revealed, too, the fact that he was only ostensibly the focus of the conflict. In reality, he was the pawn around which the weightier pieces made their moves, Philip and John positioning themselves behind and in front of him, and Constance and Eleanor taking up their stance on a diagonal line across him, as each accused the other of usurping the crown. Arthur's helplessness was further emphasised a few lines later when, on his request to Arthur to yield to him, John, who was still in the downstage centre position, knelt to Arthur and opened his arms wide, as if in homage and welcome. On her words, 'Come to thy grandam, child', Eleanor replicated John's move, so that Arthur appeared to be the one in a position of vantage. Constance's response, however, drew attention to the masquerade.

> Do, child, go to it grandam, child.
> Give grandam kingdom, and it grandam will
> Give it a plum, a cherry, and a fig.
> There's a good grandam. (160–3)

The standing figure in the centre had no power. Homage and affection were simply ploys to mask self-interest.

The verbal battle between Constance and Eleanor ended not in checkmate but in a stalemate which Hubert (a Citizen of Angiers) was summond to resolve. Played in this production by Robert Demeger in an outfit resembling that of a French onion-seller, his presence on the balcony behind the barricade of ladders provided a satiric perspective on the bickering of the kings. Physically and temperamentally, John and Philip were strongly contrasted, the former small, pugnacious and easily tiring of any form of pretence, the latter suave, elegant, an astute and able politician. Both, however, were primarily interested only in power. When Hubert enquired, 'Who is it that hath warned us to the walls?' Philip raised Arthur's arm on his reply, ''Tis France, for England', thus emphasising the fact that he spoke on Arthur's behalf. On John's angry assertion of his counter-claim, however, Philip indicated to Arthur that he should kneel facing Hubert, and then patted him benevolently and patronisingly on the head. It was a small, controlled gesture, eloquent of the authority Philip clearly felt to be vested in himself. John's expression of his claim to Angiers was unsophisticated and direct. When Hubert tried to escape the imposed role of arbitrator between Philip and John by claiming that he was the King of England's subject and would wait to demonstrate his allegiance until it was clearly established who that king in fact was, Nicholas Woodeson as John responded by rapping peremptorily on the ladders as he spoke the lines: 'Acknowledge then the King, and let me in.'

His anger grew when Hubert replied that the town would prove itself loyal to the eventual victor, but in the interim the citizens 'rammed up [their] gates against the world'. Swiftly, he held the crown that was chained to his waist out at arm's length, as he furiously enquired whether the English crown did not 'prove the King', then placed it firmly on his head. The fact that John needed to keep the crown chained to his person was an ironic comment on the security of his position as king. His small seething figure, imprisoned crown in hand, was emblematic of the future battles that would rage for that crown and within the body of John himself.

The first of those battles followed swiftly. As Hubert would not adjudicate the quarrel, John collected the massive sword from its downstage centre position (on line 283), and placed it in the centre of the stage so that it exactly bisected the playing space. In warlike mood, John and Philip then confronted each other, one on either side of the sword, while the Bastard and Austria, respectively, armoured them for the coming battle. Each side had presented its case: John was matched against Philip, Eleanor against Constance, the Bastard against Austria. Arthur was largely expendable, a small chess-piece to be moved here and there, appealed to, briefly honoured, made to kneel, to utilise his childish sincerity on his elders' behalf. As John moved to centre with the sword, he indicated brusquely that Arthur should abdicate the central position in which Philip had placed him. In the arming ceremony that followed, Arthur, exiled to the periphery of the action, was to all intents and purposes forgotten by the main combatants.

The offstage battle which follows the vaunts that make up the first movement of II.i is inconclusive. Though the French and English Heralds make the best cases they can on behalf of their respective armies, Hubert is not impressed by their claims. In the Warner production, when the representatives of the two sides returned to the stage, the mood was more sombre and downcast than it had been previously. Prior to the battle, apart from the instances when John, Eleanor and Arthur knelt, the actors remained standing throughout. The changed attitude after the military engagement was immediately apparent in the tired way in which the majority of the characters immediately sat or knelt. Again, the division between the two factions was clearly and economically presented, the English predominantly dressed in black and khaki, taking up positions stage left, the French, chiefly in beige and light brown, moving to stage right. Only the Bastard responded to events with energy and decisiveness at this point, as he put forward his suggestion that the English and French forces should unite against the recalcitrant town. The focus then shifted to the discrepancy between the Anglo-French response and that of Hubert, with the two armies huddling together around a map and then excitedly exiting as the Bastard urged them on, and Hubert, outmanoeuvred, desperately seeking for a solution to his, and the town's, peril. His proposal that Lewis should marry Blanche was made centre stage, leaning anxiously over the balcony. The Bastard, on the lower level, was also centre stage, John down left and Philip down right. The two kings, who had shaken hands on the project and were on the point of exiting, turned back to listen to Hubert and so were facing both him and the Bastard, the two instigators of solutions to break the deadlock. The Bastard was therefore in an excellent position to see the kings' faces and to realise that he had lost the debate.

Hubert's answer to the previously insoluble dilemma brought to centre stage two characters who until this point had been largely peripheral, Lewis and Blanche. Firstly, John moved to centre and held out his hand to Blanche to join him. Then, when the Dauphin crossed to Blanche, John moved away, leaving the young couple in the focal position. Where Arthur had been placed in semblance of authority, and John and Philip had prepared themselves for war, Blanche and Lewis now joined hands and lips, a union which looked back to Philip, Arthur's champion, raising the prince's hand in proof of his legitimacy, and forward to the following scene where the joining and disjoining of hands would signify the making and breaking of vows. Hubert moved the central ladders apart to allow entrance into Angiers, where the marriage would take place, and the Bastard, who had climbed up one of the ladders, stage left, as the course of events slipped from his control, now leaped down and soundly berated the self-interested actions of the kings.

The promised unity which concludes II.i is overturned in the subsequent scene. The seeds of dissension are present, in Philip's anxiety about Constance's response to the news, even as the characters prepare to celebrate the marriage of the English and French royal houses. Act III, scene i reveals the insubstantial basis on which the Anglo-French alliance is built, a fact which was demonstrated in the Warner production by the claiming by successive characters of positions of power on the playing space. Visual patterns from the previous scene, notably of kneeling or joining hands, were repeated and reworked, beginning at line 135 with the addition of another player in the power game, a new and important chess-piece who represented the papal interest – not a bishop, however, but a cardinal.

Prior to the entrance of Cardinal Pandulph, it was Constance who largely controlled the action and the performance area. Her declaration that she would 'instruct [her] sorrows to be proud' was made centre stage, and, immediately prior to her lines 'Here I and sorrows sit / Here is my throne. Bid kings come bow to it' (73–4), she sat, legs crossed in front of her, arms firmly planted on her knees. This action introduced a new visual dynamic into the piece. The minimal setting of the Warner production and the intimate relationship between actors and audience gave added meaning to the simplest of actions, so that sitting and kneeling, for example, became imbued with additional significance. In II.i these bodily positions represented either fatigue and despondency or a character's self-presentation in the role of suppliant. Constance at this point evoked neither of these sets of ideas. As she herself made clear, the ground was her throne. From this position of authority, she commanded the stage. As the wedding party entered behind her, their festive laughter died abruptly. Blanche and Lewis remained upstage centre, immediately in front of the gap in the line of ladders, hands joined, frozen into stillness, the harmony they seemingly presented negated by the vengeful, black-clad figure of Constance whose claim to her majesty in grief was confirmed when Philip crouched beside her to plead with her to see reason, thus effectively doffing his own regal mantle and laying it on her shoulders.

Constance, however, rejected Philip's attempt to placate her. As she conjured the heavens to take up arms 'against these perjured Kings', Susan Engel joined her hands piously together as though she were in a church, thus appealing over the heads of those present to a greater and divine authority. Constance's prayer is answered in the play in the figure of Cardinal Pandulph, the Pope's – and by extension, God's – representative, and, in addition, a consummate politician and power-broker. In this production he entered in the middle of an unseemly scuffle, which arose out of the Bastard's championship of Constance. On Constance's prayer to heaven to 'Set armèd discord 'twixt these perjured Kings', Austria moved towards her, counselling restraint; then stood centre stage looking extremely foolish, as Constance, who had got to her feet, circled round him, mocking his pretended courage. As he replied to Constance, Austria crossed down left, thus leaving the centre of the stage free, and taking up a position on a diagonal from the Bastard who stood up right. The sparring that had occurred between the two of them in the previous scene, and their mirror actions in arming their respective monarchs, added to the significance of what happened at this point. In silence, the Bastard moved to the central position which Austria had vacated and deliberately and contemptuously repeated Constance's words of mockery. As Austria moved towards the Bastard, as though to hit him, John ran between them, furiously pushing the Bastard out of the way. He himself was knocked over by the Bastard, and, in the general mêlée, the majority of the other characters also ended up on the floor. Pandulph's opening greeting, therefore, 'Hail, you anointed deputies of heaven!' became a sardonic comment on the incident he had just witnessed. With the exception of John and the Bastard, those present did their best to eradicate the unfortunate initial impression they had made by quickly kneeling in submission to the papal legate. The positions they took up, in two lines facing each other, close to the middle of the playing space, created the effect of a church aisle, with the result that John, who was standing between the two lines, appeared to make his defiance of the Pope while actually inside a church (a fact which the scandalised crossing of themselves by the kneeling figures emphasised).

John underlined his refusal to show allegiance to the Pope by himself making the sign of the cross only as he claimed to be 'supreme head', 'under God' alone, and not in submission to the Cardinal. As he defiantly claimed the Pope's friends as his foes, John caught hold of Philip's hand in token of the alliance between them and held it up for everyone to see. Philip was therefore in a reverse situation to that which he had been in in the previous scene when he had demonstrated his authority to Hubert by holding up Arthur's hand. Now, much against his will, he lent his hand to confirm John's legitimacy. Philip's discomfiture increased when Pandulph countered John's invective with a pronouncement of excommunication. On Pandulph's conferring of blessing on anyone who revolted from his allegiance to John, Philip tried to break the English King's hold on him, but without success. The other characters stood at this point and moved away from the centre, leaving Pandulph downstage centre facing the still physically united Philip and John. The positions of the three of them had therefore some resemblance to those of Constance, Blanche and Lewis immediately after the entrance of the wedding party, a resemblance, however, which stressed the changes in fortune which had overtaken the various characters since that point. Now, Constance's prayers had been answered through the presence of the

Cardinal, and the forcible linking of the two kings served as an ironic comment on the joined hands of Lewis and Blanche.

The seemingly simple presentation of II.i and III.i was based on immensely detailed work on the text. With only a handful of props and a stage bare of everything except a line of ladders, the actors played out the debate over who should wear the English crown. As one character after another moved to positions of dominance, a corresponding pattern of spatial relationships and gestures underlined the shifts in the power balance. In the main, power was presented satirically. John held on to his crown only by carrying it around with him chained to his waist, and alliances could be broken as easily as the disjoining of hands. The one exception to this view of power was the sequence of action in which Constance sat on the ground to claim it as her throne and Philip tacitly affirmed her authority by crouching beside her. Power in *King John* is in the hands of men. Eleanor and Constance may harangue each other on behalf of their sons, but they have little power in their own right. Like Buzz Goodbody in her 1979 Theatre-go-round production, Deborah Warner, another woman director in the male-dominated RSC, satirised male attitudes to power. Only Constance was allowed a moment of power that was not undercut.

Power, for women, can, however, be only illusory in the world *King John* depicts. In the BBC production, Blanche's costume revealed her from the start as a sacrificial victim. In the Warner version, Blanche wore an overgarment of chain-mail to show that she, too, was a soldier; but, when the fragile Anglo-French alliance was shattered, her forthrightness and determination were of no avail to her and her costume consequently became an ironic comment on the ineradicable weakness of her position. As she spoke the words 'The sun's o'ercast with blood; fair day, adieu!' the actress was kneeling. She then stood and looked helplessly around her – in turn, to Lewis, John, Philip and Eleanor – as she dissected the nightmare of conflicting loyalties in which she found herself. Lewis's view of Blanche's place in the scheme of things was simpler. On his words 'Lady, with me, with me thy fortune lies', he underlined this double affirmation by pulling her with him as he exited down left; but as Blanche completed the couplet – 'There where my fortune lives, there my life dies' – her upstage hand still reached out towards her uncle, John.

The position of Blanche at the end of the scene, central but pulled away from centre, one hand firmly joined to that of Lewis, the other reaching out to John, embodied the inconclusive nature of the chain of events at this point. Her anguished realisation that the sun is hidden by a pall of blood haunts the remainder of the play, as the relatively formal, controlled debates of the opening scenes are succeeded by the presentation of a world that is increasingly dark and bloody, and control of events slips gradually from all the characters' hands. Blanche, 'cast in the familiar female role of a medium of exchange between men', becomes, Phyllis Rackin argues, not the means of uniting the 'warring factions' but, instead, 'the embodiment of their divisions' ('Anti-historians', p. 339). The staging in the Warner production emphasised this attribute of Blanche. She is the first victim of the power battles, and her hand helplessly reaching back towards her uncle's ironically forecast the hands that would later unite in alliance – and break apart, as pledges were dishonoured.

Whose play is it? A re-examination of key characters

In interview, Deborah Warner commented that one of the difficulties she encountered with *King John*, and one of the reasons why she viewed it as benefiting from an experimental approach, is that Shakespeare has provided a number of leading characters 'whose play it might be'. Apart from John, many other characters – Constance, Pandulph, King Philip, Hubert and the Bastard – all have substantial roles. Larry S. Champion notes that King John speaks only seventeen per cent of the lines in the play (*Perspective in Shakespeare's English Histories*, p. 95), a figure he contrasts with Richard III's over thirty per cent, and Richard II's 'more than one-fourth of the total lines in his play' (*ibid.*, p. 94). In *King John* the number of lines spoken by the eponymous character is in fact bettered by the Bastard's twenty per cent. Constance speaks ten per cent of the lines, even though she appears only in the first three acts, King Philip and Hubert each eight per cent, and Pandulph six per cent, (*ibid.*, p. 95). Then, too, there is Arthur, who, though he does not have many lines, is of crucial significance within the play's action. The difficulty of deciding whose play it is is compounded by the problems John presents as the leading character: his lack of consistency and the difficulty of knowing what the motivations for his actions are. In the twentieth century, the solution has chiefly been to designate the Bastard as the play's hero as well as its major choric figure. The Warner production looked afresh at the various characters to try to discover whose play it is, and what, from a late twentieth-century perspective, its major structuring elements would seem to be.

Juliet Dusinberre identifies the difficulty of deciding what is the play's central motivating force as the source of its 'interest to feminists':

> Where does its central drive lie: where the great actress located it, in the figure of Constance? Where Hazlitt saw it, in the pathos of Arthur and the comedy of the Bastard? In the title role of John himself? Or, as some critics have claimed, in the identity of England, a nation emerging from papal domination? What is clear, from reading the play – and Deborah Warner's 1988 production reinforced this impression – is that up till the end of Act 3 the dramatic action is dominated by the women characters, and this is a cause of extreme embarrassment to the men on stage, while it also provides a pretext for their own determination to create embarrassment for those women. ('*King John* and embarrassing women', p. 40).

Attention has already been drawn to King Philip crouching on the ground beside Constance, an attitude that certainly signified his embarrassment. The following section discusses Engel's re-examination of Constance in greater detail. Other characters whose presentation contributed to the radical nature of the production are then discussed, prior to returning to an analysis of the production, this time from III.iii onwards.

Susan Engel as Constance

In her analysis of the play, Dusinberre describes Constance's lines, as she seats herself on the ground in the 'state of [her] great grief', as the 'locus for the conflict of power and power-lessness which shapes the whole play'. When discussing Constance's action (in interview), Susan Engel explained that she found sitting on the ground an easy concept to relate to 'because sitting is what you do when you protest, in Vietnam or in Westminster'. Constance was a victim of political chicanery and she sat as a political protest. It was a protest against her own treatment, and, by extension, given the twentieth-century significance of her action, a protest also which drew attention to the plight of all helpless women and other victimised groups. Constance's action at this juncture has long been established as a high point of the play. Actresses have traditionally been praised for the power they have displayed in this scene, but it has been a power based usually on Constance's role as agonised mother. Engel's Constance claimed her space of power as a woman rather than a mother. Her position centre stage was hers alone; Arthur was not beside her at this point.

Like Claire Bloom in the BBC *King John*, Susan Engel questioned the idea that Constance goes mad. Whereas Claire Bloom's performance in III.iv pointed to the discrepancy between Constance's actual state of mind and what the men misread as conventional signs of madness, Susan Engel depicted madness as an available role which Constance at times appropriated because it was the only outlet for her anger. As always, she was dressed in sombre black, relieved only by the crucifix she wore on a chain around her neck. In this scene, however, she had taken off her boots, and her bare feet and unkempt hair made her look both vulnerable and rather witch-like. Her posture, which had been very erect, seemed to have lost its equilibrium and, at moments, she raised her arms and twisted her body into an arc, so that she resembled a slowly-spinning top. Her actions at these points were characterised by a febrile and decentred inner momentum, which broke through her comparative stillness at other times. The result was a strange, dislocated dance of powerlessness in the process of which she would, for example, suddenly figure herself for a moment as an obscene and terrifying monster or kiss Pandulph's hand, as a representative of Death's 'detestable bones', in a way that accused the self-interestedness of the politically powerful men who surrounded her.

The heightened nature of Constance's language, what Engel described as 'operatic tirades', and the intensity of the character's anger and grief in the 'mad' scene, constituted a major challenge for the actress given the intimate actor/audience relationship of The Other Place, and the raw, consciously unheroic tenor of the whole production which militated against an operatic approach to character. Susan Engel was faced therefore with the problem of speaking some of the most intricate and impassioned poetry of the play, while at the same time remaining convincing as a human being to people who were sitting so close that at any moment they could have reached out and touched her. Her skill in balancing the need to give the heightened language and emotion their due weight and to present a Constance whom a modern audience, seated at close range, could believe in is attested by the reviews. 'Susan Engel hoists herself effortlessly over the syntactical assault course of her speeches', Paul Taylor commented in *The Independent* (12 May 1988), while in *The Guardian* of the same day Michael Billington praised her skill in making 'Constance, that Niagara of grief, an authentically tragic figure thrusting her face up against that of the Papal legate . . . to talk of "amiable lovely death"', and, in *The Times* (4 May 1989), Irving Wardle commended her transformation of 'the almost unplayably formalized rhetoric into living speech'.

David Morrissey as the Bastard

Susan Engel offered a reinterpretation of Constance which had a particular relevance for a late twentieth-century audience. Probably the most daring aspect of an iconoclastic production, however, was the director's decision to cast the young, relatively inexperienced David Morrissey in the role of the Bastard.

For reviewers, this was unquestionably the most contentious characterisation of the production. Charles Osborne in *The Daily Telegraph* (30 May 1988) considered that the role was 'played noisily and often incomprehensibly', and, in place of the 'ironic detachment' that he felt should characterise the Bastard, Paul Taylor in *The Independent* (12 May 1988) found 'only the detachment of a football heckler'. By contrast, however, Michael Coveney (*Financial Times*, 12 May), described Morrissey as 'a ferociously talented and watchable newcomer'.

David Morrissey's Bastard was very different from the traditional concept of the character. He was not witty or urbane, and he certainly had little or no detachment from events. He was a loud, rough, honest young man who saw the world in fairly simple terms, and, because of his simplicity and honesty, was able to act with decision and spontaneity. His idea of humour, as demonstrated soon after his first appearance, was to forcibly seat his indignant brother on his knee and use him as a ventriloquist's dummy. When his mother admitted his bastardy and named Richard I as his father, he let out a great whoop of joy. In place of the more usual interpretation of the character as an ironic commentator on a corrupt society, he played a man who, by manners and upbringing, was exterior to that society, but who threw himself wholeheartedly into it when he had the chance, and, in so doing, discovered its meannesses and compromises. He began as a noisy, endearing innocent, but the effect of the fact that he erected no barrier between himself and events was that, of all the characters in the play, he was the one who by the end appeared most notably to have undertaken an inner journey. In the 'Commodity' speech, which was an early milestone on this journey, his own lack of smoothness lent credence to his personification of 'That smooth-faced gentleman', while his vehement honesty made it not at all surprising when he failed to follow his own advice, speaking out in Constance's defence against the English interest, and refusing to kowtow to John when he disapproved of his actions.

The growth in his emotional and moral capacities was revealed most vividly in IV.iii in his reaction to the dead prince.

His admonition to Hubert to despair if he had had any part in the boy's death was made as he crouched on the floor, overcome with the horror of what had taken place. The command: 'Go, bear him in thine arms', was spoken in a voice husky with tears. The obvious sincerity of his grief, his spontaneity and the innocence he retained, alongside his growing sense both of the political manoeuvrings of the various parties and of the bewildering complexities of which he was a part, gave him the right to prophesy the effect of Arthur's death, setting one notion of England (the dead boy who had had a strong right to be king) against that of a country now left 'To tug and scramble and to part by th'teeth / The unowed interest of proud-swelling state' (IV.iii.146–7).

Though he grew in moral stature as the action progressed, Morrissey's Bastard was in no sense a conventional hero. In contrast to George Costigan's splendid costume in the BBC *John*, with its magnificent collar, and his shield bearing the emblem of the lion rampant, Morrissey, at the siege of Angiers, was draped in a cross-of-St-George banner that looked as if it had come out of a children's dressing-up box. Throughout, the production debunked any simple acceptance of heroism or patriotism. In addition, it offered a more complex reading than the frequent twentieth-century interpretation that the Bastard remains loyal to John because any king, even a bad one, is better than the danger of civil revolt. This was very much the way in which George Costigan played, for instance, the end of V.i. Morrissey's portrayal of this scene was substantially different. When he entered with the news that the lords had gone over to the French, and that John's major bargaining counter, Arthur, was dead, John collapsed to the ground, at which the Bastard crouched beside him, urging him to a policy of self-defence. The two figures, each dressed at this point in black with touches of white, presented a notable contrast, John still and helpless, the Bastard full of energy and purpose despite the desperate turn of events. When they got to their feet, John's weakness and the Bastard's strength were even more strongly pronounced. John's lack of belief in his capacity to control events was evident in the way he handled the crown. The object to which he had clung so tenaciously through all his changes of fortune now dangled from his hand, almost forgotten. As he handed over to the Bastard the power to make vital decisions ('Have thou the ordering of this present time'), he pathetically lifted up the crown slightly, as though, perhaps, to give up *all* his authority. The Bastard, however, affirmed his loyalty to his king by placing the crown on John's head, and his affection for the man by holding John's face briefly and tenderly between his two hands. Whereas Costigan showed no sympathy for John as a human being, but responded positively only to his symbolic importance as a representative of the concept of royalty, Morrissey stressed the value of affection and loyalty between human beings.

Nicholas Woodeson as John

Descriptions in newspaper accounts of Nicholas Woodeson as John suggest the satiric qualities that Emrys James brought to the character in Barton's adaptations. Irving Wardle, for example, described him as 'a jaunty tinpot monarch' (*The Times*, 4 May 1989), and Michael Billington commented that he turned up 'for the siege of Angiers looking like a visiting fireman or Dudley Moore unwontedly cast in an historical epic' (*The Guardian*, 12 May 1988). Billington also noted, however, that John and Hubert were the pivotal figures of the production, as they had 'to make the crucial transition from minor comic key to major tragic one'.

The coherence that Nicholas Woodeson found in the character stemmed from his rejection of the conventional view that John is inconsistent and untrustworthy. Unlike King Philip and Pandulph, who were skilled at manipulating words and transforming them into a smoke-screen which hid the speakers' true intentions, this John expressed his meaning directly and without guile. In interview, Nicholas Woodeson commented that he saw the character as 'a study of a very primitive form of power'. In his view, John fought to retain the kingdom because he believed, quite simply, that he had a right to be king (as much right at least as anyone else), and he demonstrated this perception by carrying the crown with him wherever he went, attached to his waist during his military campaigns. In Woodeson's portrayal, John was an essentially conservative man who saw the operations of power in simplified terms. Despite John's belief in his right to be king, there was, however, Woodeson thought, 'All the way through [the play] the psychological profile of somebody who never really was certain of his own legitimacy as a human being'. For the actor, John's crucial relationships were with Arthur and the Bastard. In the first scene, he noted, John comes face to face with the Bastard, a young man whom the text describes as physically very similar to his father, John's brother, Richard. In the next scene, John is confronted with a child who closely resembled his father, John's other elder brother, Geoffrey. John forms a lasting friendship with the Bastard, whereas his protestations of affection towards Arthur are followed by his plotting of the boy's murder. Both Arthur and the Bastard, however, are representative of legitimacy, Arthur because of the attitude of others towards him, and the Bastard because of his own confidence in his personal worth ('I am I, howe'er I was begot'). Woodeson's John lacked a robust sense of self. He existed in his kingship, in the crown he toted ostentatiously around with him, but he had little sense of personal legitimacy.

John's transitional scene from 'minor comic' to 'major tragic' key was III.iii when he wooed Hubert to Arthur's murder. In interview, Nicholas Woodeson commented on the difference between John and Richard III, noting that John, unlike Richard, has a moral structure by which he lives his life. It is when he transgresses his own moral code, through the attempted murder of Arthur, that his world begins to fall apart. Woodeson also highlighted the importance, in V.i, of John's realisation that, despite his last minute attempt to save the boy, Arthur is in fact dead: 'from that moment, John hardly says anything. We tried to stage the scene so John implodes. He doesn't explode. He's just a shell.' His demise in the last scene one reviewer likened to a cot death. Unlike Leonard Rossiter who was finally an automaton king, still mechanically making ritualised gestures of kingship, Nicholas Woodeson suggested in the final scenes a faint glimpse of the human being who might have existed if he had been able to see himself as distinct from his crown. The last scene of this production was primarily concerned not with the concept of royalty but with what it means to be a legitimate human being, a point which will be examined further in the context of a fuller discussion of that scene.

Robert Demeger as Hubert

As Michael Billington realised, the fact that the essentially humorously presented Citizen of Angiers and Hubert, the appointed murderer of Arthur, were played as one role placed the actor in a position of crucial importance with regard to the mood and rhythms of the production. Robert Demeger's performance in Act II – head swivelling repeatedly from side to side, for example, as he watched the progress of the battle, like a comic Frenchman who had unaccountably been given the task of umpire at Wimbledon – was in line with the basically satirical presentation of events in the first two acts. His delivery of Hubert's counter-suggestion to the Bastard's proposal of a joint Anglo-French attack on Angiers was also comic in its consciously hyperbolic praise of Blanche and Lewis and in the slow, measured emphasis of his solution to the problem, 'if you marry them'. Marriage is, after all, the resolution of all good comedies. Humour was not the only note of the speech, however. The character's anxiety at the turn of events was also clearly presented. His solution was obviously one that he thought up on the spur of the moment (a reading which was at once comic and urgent). As soon as he succeeded in grabbing the attention of the two kings, who were on the point of departure, he focused quickly on Blanche, but there was then a brief hesitation as he glanced rapidly around the stage in search of a suitable mate for the royal princess. His uniformly stressed, forceful rendering of the increasingly flamboyant rhetoric underlined the absurdity of the posturing of the two, evenly-matched forces while, at the same time, accentuating his own desperate plight. In the blinding scene (which is discussed in the next section), he was the linchpin in the production's accelerated change to a more sombre mood.

Salisbury (Edward Harbour) and Pembroke (Richard Bremmer)
King John can hardly be said to be Salisbury's play or Pembroke's. The two are attendant lords, characters, for the most part, at the periphery of the decision-making process. Traditionally, their decision to leave John and join the Dauphin's forces is presented critically, and contrasted with the Bastard's unswerving loyalty. Shakespeare, however, provides a perfectly justifiable reason for their defection, their belief that John has been guilty of Arthur's murder; and, in the Warner production, their action was presented as not only justifiable but also honourable. Their later decision to return to John, on learning of the Dauphin's treachery, was not depicted in such a way as to suggest that their previous actions had been misguided. In a corrupt world, they had genuinely attempted to keep faith with what was right. The fact that this was impossible was not a matter for personal shame.

For the first half of the play their time was spent in waiting on John's decisions and acting as occasional messengers, but their disquiet at many of John's actions was obvious. At the beginning of IV.ii, they put forward their views on the superfluousness of John's second coronation with force and integrity. The repetitions in the following speech by Lord Salisbury are frequently seen as unnecessary additions which weaken the force of his basic argument. If what he says is true, the argument goes, why is it necessary to constantly restate it?

> Therefore, to be possessed with double pomp,
> To guard a title that was rich before,
> To gild refinèd gold, to paint the lily,
> To throw a perfume on the violet,
> To smooth the ice, or add another hue
> Unto the rainbow, or with taper-light
> To seek the beauteous eye of heaven to garnish,
> Is wasteful and ridiculous excess. (9–16)

Edward Harbour spoke the lines, however, with passionate commitment, as a last-ditch attempt to draw John back from a foolish and dangerous course of action. There was no suggestion that he was insincere or misguided. He had silently watched John's foolish and, he now believed, murderous actions; and, when at last, he spoke out, he did so as emphatically as possible.

The Staging from III.iii onwards

Before considering the development of the action from III.iii onwards, it is useful to summarise briefly the experience the production had offered its audience up to that point. Firstly, there was the playing area itself: clean, wooden, bare, non-representational, an empty space for the construction of significance; then, the lighting, for a large percentage of the time very bright and open, exposing the shoddy dealings and broken promises. Throughout, the stress was on the theatricality of the event, whether the lighting was hard and white and revealing, or, for example, when the ladders created a wonderful floor-texture of shadows or the spotlit balcony provided Hubert with a vantage-point for his splendidly comic umpiring of the first battle. The floor, tennis-court, bullring, chess board, was infinitely adaptable. Upon it, successive images and momentary tableaux encapsulated the production's attitude as it interpreted the play's narrative and meaning.

As the audience entered, Chatillon, the French Ambassador, walked to and fro across the performance space. When the lights went down, he continued pacing, ignominiously waiting for John to appear and hear his message from King Philip. Almost a minute after the start of the performance, Salisbury and Pembroke entered and waited also, silently watching Chatillon. The slow, wary atmosphere that was established in the opening moments was suddenly broken by the speedy entry of John and Eleanor. There was no suggestion of the pomp and ceremony of a court room. John's only semblance of majesty was his crown, and the two lords wore mud-stained coats. At this makeshift court the simplest of props sufficed to present the mood of characters or changes of fortune: John expressed his anger towards Chatillon by furiously throwing the contents of a cup of water at his retreating back, and he knighted the Bastard by placing a white scarf round his shoulders. The performance style in the first two acts had a strip-cartoon-like quality which punctured the pomposity and self-interest of the characters. Act III, scene i was generally portrayed in the same vein (with the exception of Constance's moment of power), but the ending was darker, introducing a different perspective into the action.

At the start of III.iii, the gods seemingly are with John: he has been victorious in battle, and has captured Arthur. Nicholas Woodeson played John as exultantly gleeful at this point, his attitude to Arthur self-consciously jolly and avuncular. In a presumably unconscious parody (on the character's part) of his act of submission in kneeling to Arthur in II.i, he crouched in front of the boy, tousling his hair and pinching his cheeks, in between looking around at the other characters to see whether they appreciated his role of good-natured uncle. Arthur stood, ill at ease but submissive, as John went on to stand behind him, tickle him under the arms and waggle his ears, grinning all the while. At last, however, Arthur could bear being mauled about no longer and, as John's hand came round to tickle his chest, he sank his teeth into it, at which, without a moment's hesitation, John karate-chopped his shoulder so that he fell to the floor. The lack of premeditation in the action was symptomatic of Warner's interpretation. John was angry, so he hit out. His previous show of affection for Arthur was inept. Far from being a Machiavellian schemer, this John had no skill in dissembling.

The duologue in which John persuades Hubert to agree to Arthur's death was played on the balcony. On her line, 'Come hither, little kinsman. Hark, a word', Eleanor took Arthur aside and sat down with him on the floor. John was therefore left by himself, at a loose end, and so he, in his turn, called Hubert to him. He began his circumlocutory approach to the desired killing on the main stage area, but, following his initial words of gratitude and affection to Hubert, he went up, in silence, on to the balcony. For a moment, Hubert stood, at a loss, and then followed after John. The lights went out on the lower area, leaving only the balcony lit, and with the lighting change came a change of mood. With passionate intensity, John whispered to Hubert: 'I had a thing to say – but let it go.' The narrow beam of light which created their isolated refuge John transformed, through low-pitched, rapid speech, into a graveyard, a dark and silent place, where, without the aid of eyes or ears, by mental processes alone, Hubert could grasp his meaning. His words of love to Hubert, after the latter had agreed to the murder, were spoken very gently, almost plaintively. John returned to the lower stage before Hubert and looked up at him in a way that was both complicit and tender, as he placed his finger on his lips and urged Hubert to remember the pact between them. A moment on the balcony, however, before John returned to the main stage area, revealed another aspect of the king. After promising Hubert a future reward, though notably failing to specify what form this reward would take, John turned to leave, but his exit was a false one, for he immediately returned to collect the crown which he had momentarily left slung over a ladder. The implication was not that John had presented Hubert with a dishonest show of friendship: while the terrible need for Arthur's death burned within him, he genuinely loved the future means of that death. But once the interview was over, his focus was again on his constant prop, the crown. Only when that was safely under his control could his thoughts revert to his promise to Hubert.

The more sombre mood indicated by Blanche at the end of III.i, and continued by John and Hubert, was carried through into Constance's final scene in III. iv. When she exited, Philip went after her and the Dauphin threw his elegant fawn-coloured coat on the ground, centre. A few lines later, he sat down on it, in a position that was at once arrogant and petulant. At first, he turned fiercely and pettishly away from Pandulph's attempts to persuade him to continue the war against John, despite the recent defeat of the French forces. Gradually, however, he was won round. As Pandulph forged the most horrifying chain in the reasoning which he employed to incite the Dauphin to action (the certainty that, should Arthur still be alive at that point, John would murder him when he heard of the approach of the Dauphin's troops, and the indignant English would then revolt from their allegiance to John), he knelt close to Lewis, a father confessor exhorting his spiritual son to perform his religious duty. At the conclusion of the scene, both men were standing. Pandulph picked up the coat of his now dutiful and obedient 'son' and placed it round his shoulders, an action at once protective and patronising, which emphasised his power over Lewis and echoed Eleanor's whispered advice to *her* son in the first scene regarding the priority of might over right, and also Constance's embraces of Arthur.

The BBC *King John* emphasised the contrast between the Pandulph/Lewis scene and the Hubert/Arthur scene by playing them without a break, whereas the Warner production took an interval between the two scenes. The lighting for IV.i, the projected blinding of Arthur, was in marked contrast to that of the first half of the play. Only one large lamp was used, and this was mounted on the balcony edge. Only the playing space occupied by Hubert and Arthur was lit and the effect was harsh and cold. Hubert entered in silence and opened a trapdoor. The executioner then came in, still in silence, and placed a bundle containing the instruments of torture on the floor, centre. With expert precision, Hubert tested out the various instruments and finally chose a double-pronged one, with which he had first practised the act of blinding someone. He then spoke the first words of the scene, 'Heat me these irons hot', stressing 'these', and so emphasising the decision he had just made. A further use of props (and costumes) later in the scene clarified important stages in the relationship between gaoler and prisoner. When Arthur reminded Hubert of acts of kindness he had done for him, notably lending him his handkerchief to soothe his head when it ached, Hubert threw the handkerchief back at him. Though the intention may have been to get rid of it as quickly as possible, it became a token, for Hubert and the audience, of the innocent affection which Arthur had shown him, and the increasing impossibility of carrying out the act of mutilation. (As Michael Billington noted, 'How can you kill someone who has lent you their hankie?') The actual decision to save the boy was signalled by Hubert's relieving his pent-up feelings by hitting Arthur on the shoulder with the glove with which he would have handled the hot irons, and then kneeling beside him, weeping. When the two exited, Hubert placed his coat around Arthur to warm and protect him.

Hubert's action at this point recalled Pandulph's at the end of the previous scene, with the effect that the Warner production, like the BBC *King John*, underlined the difference between the supposedly paternal attitude of Pandulph and Hubert's genuine feeling. In addition to his role as father confessor in the play, Pandulph also represents 'mother Church'. Immediately after his first entrance, he enquiries why John 'against the church, our holy mother / So wilfully dost spurn' (III.i.141–2), and, when Philip hesitates about whether to break faith with John, Pandulph warns that if he fails to champion the Church's cause 'the church, our mother, [will] breathe her curse / A mother's curse, on her revolting son' (256–7). In the Warner production, Pandulph (played at The Other Place by Antony Brown, and The Pit by Julian Curry), in his own person, took on some of the attributes of that mother whose parental authority he repre-sented as he cajoled the reluctant Dauphin to continue his fight against John. His dismissive attitude, as he placed the Dau-phin's coat round the young man's shoulders, was contrasted with Hubert's use of his own coat, warm, all-enveloping, a pledge of his determination to protect the boy.

In the second half of the play, when the women had disap-peared from the action, the maternal function was divided between Pandulph (whose portrayal by Antony Brown at Strat-ford Michael Billington described as 'a beautiful study in steely sophistry'), as self-styled spokesperson for a controlling mother, and Hubert and the Bastard, who took on the at-tributes of nurturance and tenderness at key moments towards, respectively, Arthur and John. As has been previously noted, Morrissey's portrayal of the Bastard's loving care for John, the man, distinguished his interpretation from Costigan's. The Warner production used the absence of the women in the second half of the play to explore, through male characters, aspects of the mother–child relationship. Pandulph was a controlling mother figure, but Hubert offered Arthur loving protection, and the Bastard tenderly raised John to his feet when he fell to the floor like a helpless child.

At the start of IV.ii, Pembroke and Salisbury had the stage to themselves. Slowly and methodically, they used the few objects around them to create a new setting, placing two wooden trestles towards the rear of the stage, and then collecting one of the ladders and arranging it on top of the trestles to make a long narrow table. Around this they placed the wooden chairs that until this point had been hanging from beneath the balcony, took off their coats, placed them on the two chairs, right and left of the table, as though to reserve their places, and retired downstage – to wait. After a few moments, the sound of singing was heard, not words but 'po po po pom'. This was John, who now entered, crown rakishly at an angle. He took off his coat, placed it at the back of the central chair, and sat down. After the words 'Here once again we sit', he giggled, and on 'once again crowned' he cockily tilted the crown a little further to the side. His inability to deal adequately with the mounting pressure of events was shown in his violent swings of mood, and in his use of the crown. The fact that he was inept at the art of dissembling was evident in his response to the lords' anger at the rumour of Arthur's death, for, though he claimed to sympathise with their anxiety, he was clearly pleased to be rid of the child. When they refused to be appeased, however, and deserted him, his comment, 'They burn in indignation. I repent', was spoken with a sincere horror, and as though the indignation that fuelled the lords was contagious and scorched him inwardly. For John, the reported death of Arthur, the departure of the lords and the news which he receives immediately after this of the death of his mother were all interlinked. He responded to the Messenger's tidings of the imminent French invasion with fury, but, on hearing of the loss of his mother, and also therefore of a powerful ally to watch over his interests in France, he took off the crown, and sat, giddy and afraid, on a chair in front of the table. He did not put the crown back on his head until Peter of Pomfret's prophecy that, on the next Ascension Day, he would give up his crown, a reappropriation which demonstrated his determination to hold fast to the realm come what may.

John's only words of soliloquy – 'My mother dead!' – were spoken whilst he was seated upstage centre behind the table. They were preceded by one of the few lengthy pauses in the production, and were delivered with a sense of desperation, almost of anguish, as though John, the man without a sense of personal legitimacy, was now truly bereft. In the subsequent interchange with Hubert, his rage at his inability to contain the disorder that threatened him burst out uncontrollably. As Hubert described the bizarre and fearful apparitions in the heavens that had reputedly followed news of Arthur's death, and the prophecies of dire future occurrences that these gave rise to, John sat, as though at his ease, lolling back in his chair, with his feet on the table. His first words in reply were spoken quietly, if ominously, but then, in one swift movement, he was on his feet, knocking over the ladder that constituted the table, and drawing a lethal-looking knife from his boot. As he did so, he excoriated Hubert as the villain who had reacted to his whim of the moment as though it were 'a warrant / To break within the bloody house of life', and murder the young prince.

After the drawing of the knife, John's changes in mood occurred with lightning speed. When Hubert showed him his own warrant authorising the execution, he gave a terrible cry and rushed away from it. He was almost in tears as he claimed that, if Hubert had only hesitated when he broached the subject of Arthur's death, 'Deep shame' would have 'struck [him] dumb'. Only six lines later, as he evoked 'The deed which both our tongues held vile to name', he picked up a chair, as though to hurl it at Hubert, but then threw it to the floor and sank helplessly down himself, on his description of the 'civil tumult' within him. When Hubert told him, however, that Arthur was still alive, all the anguish and horror were forgotten. The boy was safe after all, so there was no longer any cause for recrimi-nations. Belatedly, he offered an apology to Hubert for the unfounded accusations he had made against him, but Woodeson's offhand delivery belied any suggestion that John might feel genuine compunction for his harsh comments. Two actions involving his constant prop, the crown, at the end of this scene further revealed his state of mind. After repudiating the notion that he would butcher an innocent child, Hubert crum-pled the warrant and threw it at John's feet, whereupon John placed the crown over it before picking it up, and, with the other hand, returned the knife to his boot. Thus, in one brief moment, he reasserted his royal status, appropriated the docu-ment which could yet testify against him, and put away the weapon which, for the moment at least, he no longer needed in self-defence. Before he exited, he threw the crown from one hand to the other, as though reliving the jaunty mood of the beginning of the scene, then ran quickly off the stage, whether away from danger or to prepare for it was uncertain.

During the interval a ladder had been positioned so that it projected from upstage centre of the balcony, above the playing space, and this was used for Arthur's leap from the battlements. Only Arthur and the ladder were visible in the surrounding blackness, so that, when he jumped, it appeared to be into a void. From this point in the play onwards, echoing the increas-ing sense of fragmentation, the lighting changes were more frequent and sudden, brightly-lit scenes alternating with others played in semi-darkness. Patterns of significance established in the first part of the play concerning the crucial importance of loyalty, the making – and breaking – of vows, were continued and reworked in the later scenes. After the discovery of Arthur's body, Salisbury and Pembroke knelt, one each side of him, and pledged themselves to avenge his death. Pembroke then covered Arthur's face with his coat. The image the group made was echoed in V.iv when Pembroke and Salisbury again knelt, this time by the dying Melun, and Salisbury took off his coat and placed it under Melun's head to ease his final agonised moments. It was an action which contained another echo also,

[131]

that of Hubert placing his coat protectively around Arthur at the end of IV. i. The vow the lords made on Arthur's body found a reformulation in the tableau at the beginning of V.ii when Lewis stood upstage centre, and Salisbury and Pembroke ceremoniously placed their hands on his in token of allegiance (see illustrations). This vow, however, unlike the one made over Arthur's body, recalled the joining and disjoining of hands in II.i and III.i. In particular, their positioning in the playing space brought to mind the newly married Blanche and Lewis, and the violent divisions that had succeeded that union. The V.ii tableau, therefore, prefigured Lewis's future treacherous conduct when he would repay Salisbury's and Pembroke's loyalty by plotting their deaths.

At the end of IV.iii the Bastard crouched on the floor near the dead body of Arthur and wept. Arthur and the Bastard, the two signifiers for John of legitimacy, are cousins. Arthur had been imprisoned by the king because of the threat he represented, whereas the Bastard, the other nephew, had been promoted to a position of honour. Now the two of them were placed in close proximity, the play's most innocent victim lying dead, the usually ebullient young man overwhelmed with grief. When John collapsed to the floor at the end of the next scene, and the Bastard crouched beside him before helping him to his feet, their physical relationship echoed that of the Bastard and the dead Arthur in IV.iii. Now, though, the Bastard had regained his sense of purpose, and he gently, but fervently, urged John to rally the English forces against the French. For John, however, it was too late. Nothing remained of his previous belief in himself as king.

In V.iii, when John entered from the smoky battlefield, cold, blue backlighting cast shadows from the ladders across the acting area. He stood as though in a daze, coatless, in shirt sleeves, his crown unheeded in his hand. As the sound of an exploding shell was heard, Hubert ran in and pushed John down, out of danger's way. The cold eeriness of the short scene was particularly pronounced at The Other Place, where, until the worsening weather made this impossible, the large double doors facing the main entrance remained open throughout. The smoke, the noise of whizz-bangs, the darkness outside the theatre and John's bewildered figure surrounded by imprisoning shadows conjured up a surrealistic First World War image that gave form to the inward process that was destroying the king, as well as the external forces that tore apart the land. At the end of the scene, John almost fell once again, but he was caught by Hubert and the Messenger who made a chair for him with their arms and carried him out.

The final scenes of the play present a world increasingly on the point of disintegration. Pandulph, Lewis and the Bastard still attempt to control events, but their efforts meet with little success. In the Warner production, Pandulph, the play's most authoritative controlling figure, had arrived in III.i. at a moment of potential destruction of the recently achieved accord between the French and the English, and had firmly taken control of the situation. He had walked into a brawl, and the horrified combatants had scrambled to present themselves in suitable postures of piety. In V.ii, by contrast, he entered to find Lewis and the English lords with hands joined in token of their newly-found amity, and this time the characters refused to do his bidding.

Act V scene ii is also the scene of direct confrontation between the Bastard and Lewis. After the production transferred to The Pit, the Bastard gained a new and more elegant costume for the later scenes of the play. In V.ii, with his shiny breastplate neatly fitted over a long, elegant coat, he looked almost as well dressed as Lewis. At both venues, the two young men were, in addition, loudly confident – even at this stage of hostilities – to win. Two later scenes, however, demonstrated the difficulties that beset them. In V.v, Lewis ran headlong on to the stage and leaped on to the ladders at the back of the playing space. Triumphantly, he shushed the drums that had underlined his entrance, and began, publicly, to announce his success in battle; but at the height of his description a messenger entered with news of French losses on Goodwin Sands, and Lewis jumped angrily down from his position of vantage.

Act V scene vi, the duologue between Hubert and the Bastard, which establishes the fact of John's poisoning and the loss of a substantial part of the Bastard's forces, was played in darkness. John's poisoning by a monk is not prepared for in Shakespeare's play. It is announced without prior warning, and no further comment is made on it. The Bastard's losses, like Lewis's, are not the result of any miscalculation on his part, or, at least, if so, the audience are not told of this. Success or failure, life or death, appear random, as their causes are off-stage, and only partially comprehensible. The Bastard and Hubert represent, however, the strongest strand of steadfast-ness and integrity in the play's complex web of dissonances and betrayals. The positions of the two characters in this scene were discernible only by the narrow pinpoints of light from the storm lanterns they carried. The thin tracery of light they drew upon the darkness was a fitting comment on the impenetrability of the pattern of events by this point, in relation to the tiny but vital sources of illumination which the two men represented.

For the final scene, the playing area was again fully lit, though the effect was softer than it had been earlier in the play, and the pacing of the scene was slower, more reflective, than what had gone before. John was carried on to the stage in Salisbury's arms, a white blanket carefully wrapped round him, one hand outside the blanket feebly holding the crown. Salisbury placed John on the floor, centre stage, and Henry, Salisbury, Pembroke and Bigot sat or crouched nearby, unable to halt the course of the fever which ravaged the king. Most of John's lines were spoken quietly and fatalistically, as though his voice was fading like the 'scribbled form' he designates himself, but his response to his son Prince Henry's question regarding how he fared, 'Poisoned – ill fare!', was delivered with full conscious-ness of the words' irony, and his reply to Henry's wish that his tears might give his father comfort was vehement and anguished.

> The salt in them is hot.
> Within me is a hell, and there the poison
> Is as a fiend confined to tyrannize
> On unreprievable, condemnèd blood. (45–8)

The actual moment of his death passed unnoticed, and the lords pulled the blanket over his face and placed the crown on top of the recumbent form. The man who had had such difficulty in believing in his substance as a human being was gone. All that remained was the symbol of his kingship, the crown he had cherished in lieu of an inner self.

From first to last, John's changing fortunes had been signified by his relationship to his crown. In France, he had carried it chained to his body, a permanent attribute of his physical self. Briefly, he had forgotten it as he raised with Hubert the question of Arthur's death, but, once this was settled to his satisfaction, he scuttled back to reclaim it from the ladder over which he had hung it. After his second coronation, he jauntily tilted it to the side of his head in affirmation of the fact that it was now more securely his. Later in the scene, when he heard of his mother's death, he took off the crown, as though Eleanor's demise made him lose all sense of purpose; but when Peter of Pomfret prophesied that he would give up the crown, he swiftly replaced it on his head. At the end of the scene he signified his authority to do what he pleased with the warrant Hubert had thrown at his feet by surrounding it with the crown before picking it up, and, as he exited, he tossed the crown gleefully from one hand to another. His coronation by Pandulph at the beginning of V.i he treated as a charade which had to be gone through, but which in no way compromised his previous right to the crown. The news of Arthur's death, however, and the rapid advance of the French forces caused him to collapse to the floor, the crown unheeded in his hand. When the Bastard replaced it on his head, he barely responded. In the battlefield scene he stood helplessly, a small, lost figure, surrounded by smoke and distorted shadows, the crown in his hand once again forgotten. After his death, the blanket he was wrapped in was adjusted so that it covered his face, and the crown was placed on top of the blanket. It was a telling image of the end result of a disputed and destructive power. The still white bundle on the floor seemed blank, annulled, the crown appearing to rest on vacancy.

In the final scene, Shakespeare unexpectedly produces a hitherto unheard of heir to the throne of England. In the Warner *King John*, however, Jo James as Henry had already appeared in two previous roles (Robert Faulconbridge, and a messenger to King John), and was therefore established in the minds of the members of the audience as part of the world of the play. The fact that he was not an unknown entity, produced like a rabbit from a magician's hat, focused attention on his humanity rather than his future kingship. A slight, hesitant figure who never took up a position centre stage, he promised neither the certainty of future security nor the inevitability of continued strife. When the Bastard and the lords knelt in submission to him, the swaddled figure of John provided an echo of an earlier death – that of Arthur, his face also covered, in this case by the coat Pembroke had laid over him. Hubert's vow of innocence over Arthur's body was genuine, and the English lords had done their best to fulfil the promise of vengeance they had made to the dead child. Throughout, the production had drawn attention to the play's exploration of vows honoured and vows betrayed. The promises made over Arthur's body had been honoured. There was a reasonable chance, therefore, that the pledges of loyalty offered at the end of the play would be honoured also. In the final moments of the performance a group of fallible human beings who had been caught up in nightmarish events attempted to achieve a degree of reconciliation and renewal. It was a small, tentative beginning, but, in the light of what had gone before, the maximum possible – a small, still point after the often bewildering speed of complex and confused events.

Unlike the BBC production, the Warner *King John* did not end on an heroic note. The Bastard spoke the final lines kneeling in the down left corner of the playing space, while John's shrouded body with its hollow symbol of kingship lay centre stage. The production had been centrally concerned with the question of legitimacy, initially whose head should rightly wear the English crown, but increasingly of what it means to be a true human being. Throughout, John had lacked a sense of personal legitimacy. The Bastard, by contrast, who, from the beginning had had a sense of personal worth, developed an enriched understanding of the worth and needs of others. His final, quiet, but deeply felt progression towards the word 'true' disproved Pandulph's axiom that 'It is religion that doth make vows kept' (III.i.279). It discounted, too, the traditional view that the Bastard's loyalty to his king – despite John's manifold inadequacies – is the mainstay of his character. Loyalty had been revealed as an attribute of personal feeling, not religious or patriotic fervour: legitimacy as a human being was what finally counted.

In conclusion

'Naught shall make us rue / If England to itself do rest but true': these are the final words of the play. What precisely, however, is England, and what does truth to England consist of? Throughout *King John*'s stage history the concept of 'England' and the truth attendant on this has gone through a number of modifications. The first recorded production of the play took place in the context of Cibber's attempt to stage his own version in which he aimed to 'inspirit [Shakespeare's] King *John* with a resentment that justly might become an *English* monarch'. In *Papal Tyranny* England represents the forces of right, a stalwart Protestantism which is pitted against the treachery of Catholic Rome. For some theatre practitioners and audiences Shakespeare's own play has been patriotic enough, especially in times of national danger, though John Philip Kemble thought it wise to add lines of his own pointing the need to 'Sweep off [the] base invaders from the land'. Planché, Macready and their imitators used the play as a means to recreate the past, faithfully presenting on stage the visible externals of John's England. In addition, Macready established an interpretation of the character of John which was considered historically accurate and which greatly influenced later actors in the role.

In the twentieth century the question of what being true to England means has been central to the arguments of those critics who have found *King John* thematically unified. For some interpreters of the play England is the Elizabethan world of which Shakespeare was part. Being true to England meant being true to the monarch of England, Elizabeth, in order to avert the danger of attack from abroad and civil unrest at home. A linked view of the play finds a coherence of perspective in the opposed fortunes of the Bastard and John, the former rising in moral stature as the latter falls. The Bastard therefore acts as a structural device which unifies the fragmented second half of the play. He is the conscience of England, and he fittingly speaks the final words of the play. In the main, this is the way in which theatre companies have interpreted the play, at least until the later years of the century. Michael Hordern, the 1953 Old Vic King John, for example, was for many people who saw him 'an entirely adequate symbol of kingship', given the desperate need of giving unity and purpose to a country faced with internal dissent and the danger of foreign invasion. Muriel St Clare Byrne, writing of Douglas Seale's 1957 Stratford Memorial Theatre production, suggested that, once Arthur is dead, John becomes the legitimate king, and, following this restitution of 'royal *mystique*', the Bastard is able to speak on behalf of the 'national theme and make the Monarch the rallying point for national unity'.

In the opinion of Douglas C. Wixson, *King John* consists of several pieces of a puzzle which we are invited to assemble for ourselves. 'By refusing particular views Shakespeare encourages us to devise our own.' The play shifts in meaning depending on the perspective from which it is viewed. Assemble the pieces in one way and in the centre of the picture is the heroic figure of the Bastard whose love of England and belief in the concept of royalty gives focus (as in the BBC version) to everything around him. Reassemble them, however, and the bright, shiny pieces no longer interlock neatly. Instead of a picture of England worthy of patriotic fervour, the dark-coloured, jagged pieces no longer fit together properly, and the fragmented picture represents a world in which a child is reprieved, but dies anyway; battles are won and lost from causes beyond the control of commanders; and death comes without warning at the hands of an unknown assassin.

In the mid-1970s John Barton considered that the pieces could not be joined together and added others of his own, in addition to pre-existing pieces by Bale and the author of *The Troublesome Reign*. The picture he created was unified but fatalistic. Power was shown as irredeemably corrupt and the Bastard's final words of hope were so remote from actuality that they could be expressed only as a pious fiction. The Warner production, which presented Shakespeare's text uncut, offered a new perspective on the often-expressed view that the play is incoherent. The pieces did not always fully interconnect, but the gaps between them created a picture of power with considerable relevance to the late twentieth-century context of the production. Power in the Warner *King John* was male-defined, sometimes ludicrous, often cruel and inherently unstable. Kings strutted and bellowed, but their absurdity did not lessen the suffering of their victims. The production highlighted the powerlessness of women. Though Blanche wore the costume of a soldier, she was unable to escape her status as victim. Constance, in her final scene, found that the role of madwoman was her only available means of expressing her anger. Constance and Blanche, however, also demonstrated the instability of the structures that confined them. Blanche's physical and emotional situation, pulled in a variety of directions by conflicting loyalties, prophesied the brutal divisions that would destroy some of the characters and threaten them all. When Susan Engel's Constance sat on the ground in defiance of the might of kings, the fact that she did so as a political protest placed her action within the context of the present-day world and allied the plight of the individual woman in the play to that of modern groups marginalised from the centres of power. The lords had spent a good deal of their time waiting at the periphery, never at the centre of events. Eventually they spoke and acted on their own behalf, and, though they misread the situation, the rightness of their decisions was not questioned. In addition to Hubert's protection of Arthur in Shakespeare's play, the Bastard was portrayed as responding tenderly to John, and, in the final scene, Salisbury carried John in his arms, swaddled like a baby. Though power – and its abuse – was controlled by men, the fact that men were also depicted as capable of acting as nurturers undermined the masculine codes underpinning the hierarchies of power.

The final piece of the puzzle was the one which proved the most difficult to integrate within a neat, coherent whole. The lack, however, of any clear sense of dramatic closure was further evidence of the play's contemporary significance. The ending resisted the traditional view that the Bastard's words are a rallying call to a belief in the power of nationhood. Instead, following the fading away of John's 'scribbled form', the remaining characters began their hesitant search for a new beginning. It was a beginning fraught with dangers, the gaps that had been established in the traditional concept of power a source of anxiety as well as hope. In its pieces and the connections between them, the Warner production revealed *King John* as a play that explores issues crucial to our *fin-de-siècle* world: the relationship between those in possession and the dispossessed; what it means to have, and use, power legitimately; what, ultimately, it means to be a true human being.

Deborah Warner's 'wild, searching', experimental approach resulted in a production that demonstrated *King John*'s relevance to today. It may be that, after its relegation throughout much of the twentieth century to the status of a rarely performed 'stinker', the twenty-first century will look on it with more favour. In its heyday of nineteenth-century popularity, productions represented the world of *King John* as remote and picturesque. Future productions may well concentrate on what the Warner production demonstrated about the play: its search, in the face of barely-averted catastrophe, for a foundation upon which a new and, just possibly, a better world might be built.

BIBLIOGRAPHY

Allen, Shirley S., *Samuel Phelps and Sadler's Wells Theatre*, Middletown, Connecticut, 1971.

The BBC TV Shakespeare, King John, London, 1986.

Beaurline, L. A., ed., *King John* (New Cambridge Shakespeare), Cambridge, 1990.

Bonjour, Adrien, 'The road to Swinstead Abbey: a study of the sense and structure of *King John*', *English Literary History*, XVIII, 1951, 253–74.

Braunmuller, A. R., ed., *King John* (Oxford Shakespeare), Oxford, 1989.

Byrne, Muriel St Clare, 'The Shakespeare season at the Old Vic, 1956–57 and Stratford-upon-Avon, 1957', *Shakespeare Quarterly*, VIII, 1957, 463–92.

Calderwood, James L., 'Commodity and honour in *King John*', *University of Toronto Quarterly*, XXIX, 1960, 341–56, reprinted in *Shakespeare The Histories*, ed., Eugene M. Waith, Englewood Cliffs, New Jersey, 1965, 85–101.

Chambers, Colin, *Other Spaces*, London, 1980.

Champion, Larry S., *Perspective in Shakespeare's English Histories*, Athens, Georgia, 1980.

Cibber, Colley, *The Dramatic Works*, vol. V, New York, 1966.

David, Richard, 'Actors and scholars: a view of Shakespeare in the modern theatre', *Shakespeare Survey*, XII, 1959, 76–87.

Dusinberre, Juliet, '*King John* and embarrassing women', *Shakespeare Survey*, XLII, 1989, 37–52.

Evans, Gareth Lloyd, *Shakespeare II*, Edinburgh, 1969.

Fielding, Henry, *The Historical Register for the Year 1736*, ed. William W. Appleton Regents Restoration Drama Series, London, 1968.

Genest, John, ed., *Some Account of the English Stage from the Restoration in 1660 to 1830*, vol. IV, Bath, 1832.

Grennan, Eamon, 'Shakespeare's satirical history: a reading of *King John*', *Shakespeare Studies*, XI, 1978, 21–37.

Honigmann, E. A. J., ed., *King John* (Arden Shakespeare), London, 1967.

McClellan, Kenneth, *Whatever Happened to Shakespeare?*, London, 1978.

Manvell, Roger, *Shakespeare and the Film*, South Brunswick and New York, 1971.

Martin, Theodore, *Helena Faucit*, Edinburgh and London, 1900.

Odell, George C. D., *Shakespeare – from Betterton to Irving*, vol. II, London, 1920.

Planché, James Robinson, *Recollections and Reflections*, London, 1872.

Rackin, Phyllis, 'Anti-historians: women's roles in Shakespeare's histories', *Theatre Journal*, XXXVII, 1985, 329–44.

Scott, Mark W., and Williamson, Sandra L., *Shakespearean Criticism*, vol. IX, Detroit, Michigan, 1989.

Shattuck, Charles H., ed., *William Charles Macready's King John*, Urbana, Illinois, 1962.

Smallwood, R. L., ed., *King John* (New Penguin Shakespeare), Harmondsworth, 1974.

Smallwood, R. L., 'Shakespeare at Stratford-upon-Avon, 1988', *Shakespeare Quarterly*, XL, 1989, 83–96.

Smallwood, R. L., 'Shakespeare unbalanced: the Royal Shakespeare Company's *King John*, 1974–5', *Deutsche Shakespeare-Gesellschaft West Jahrbuch*, 1976, 79–99.

Smidt, Kristian, *Unconformities in Shakespeare's History Plays*, London and Basingstoke, 1982.

Sprague, Arthur Colby, *Shakespeare and the Actors*, Cambridge, Massachusetts, 1945.

Sprague, Arthur Colby, *Shakespeare's Histories*, London, 1964.

Thomson, Peter, 'A necessary theatre: the Royal Shakespeare season 1970 reviewed', *Shakespeare Survey*, XXIV, 1971, 117–26.

Thomson, Peter, 'The smallest season: the Royal Shakespeare Company at Stratford in 1974', *Shakespeare Survey*, XXVIII, 1975, 137–48.

Trewin, J. C., *Shakespeare on the English Stage*, London, 1964.

Vaughan, Virginia Mason, 'Between tetralogies: *King John* as transition', *Shakespeare Quarterly*, XXXV, 1984, 407–20.

Vickers, Brian, ed., *Shakespeare, The Critical Heritage*, vol. III, London, 1975.

Waith, Eugene M., '*King John* and the drama of history', *Shakespeare Quarterly*, XXIX, 1978, 192–211.

Williamson, Jane, *Charles Kemble, Man of the Theatre*, Lincoln, Nebraska, 1970.

Wilson, John Dover, ed., *King John*, Cambridge, 1969.

[142]

Winter, William, *Shakespeare on the Stage*, New York and London, 1916.

Wixson, Douglas C., '"Calm words folded up in smoke": propaganda and spectator response in Shakespeare's *King John*', *Shakespeare Studies*, XIV, 1981, 111–27.

Wood, Roger and Clarke, Mary, *Shakespeare at the Old Vic*, London, 1954.

APPENDIX

Principal casting of the twentieth-century productions discussed

Old Vic Theatre, 1953

Directed by George Devine
Costumes and décor by Motley

King John	Michael Hordern	*Constance*	Fay Compton
Queen Elinor	Viola Lyel	*Lymoges, Duke of Austria*	
Salisbury	Robert Hardy		Laurence Hardy
Bigot	Maxwell Gardiner	*Lord Melun*	James Maxwell
Essex	Neville Teede	*Blanche of Castile*	Gwen Cherrell
Pembroke	John Dearth	*1st Citizen of Angiers*	
Chatillon	David William		Ronald Hines
Philip the Bastard		*Hubert de Burgh*	Edgar Wreford
	Richard Burton	*French Herald*	John Lamin
Robert Faulconbridge		*English Herald*	Michael Ramsey
	Timothy Bateson	*Cardinal Pandulph*	Paul Daneman
Lady Faulconbridge		*1st Executioner*	Robert Gillespie
	Nancye Stewart	*2nd Executioner*	Robin Barbary
James Gurney	Jeremy Geidt	*Peter of Pomfret*	Timothy Bateson
King Philip	William Squire	*Prince Henry*	John Greenwood
Lewis, the Dauphin	John Neville		
Arthur, Duke of Bretagne			
	Nicky Edmett		

Stratford-upon-Avon, 1957

Directed by Douglas Seale
Scenery and costumes designed by Audrey Cruddas

King John	Robert Harris	*King Philip*	Cyril Luckham
Chatillon	Peter Cellier	*Blanch of Spain*	Doreen Aris
Queen Elinor	Molly Tapper	*A Citizen of Angiers*	
Essex	Antony Brown		Patrick Wymark
Philip, the Bastard	Alec Clunes	*A French Herald*	Thane Bettany
Robert Faulconbridge		*An English Herald*	Peter Palmer
	James Wellman	*Salisbury*	Donald Eccles
Lady Faulconbridge		*Cardinal Pandulph*	Mark Dignam
	Stephanie Bidmead	*Hubert*	Ron Haddrick
Gurney	Rex Robinson	*A Gaoler*	Julian Glover
Lewis the Dauphin	Barry Warren	*Pembroke*	Robin Lloyd
Arthur, Duke of Bretagne		*A Messenger*	Derek Mayhew
	Christopher Bond	*Peter of Pomfret*	William Elmhirst
Lymoges, Duke of Austria		*Bigot*	Donald Layne-Smith
	Clive Revill	*Melun*	Toby Robertson
Constance	Joan Miller	*Prince Henry*	Gordon Wright

Stratford-upon-Avon, 1974

Directed by John Barton with Barry Kyle
Designed by John Napier with Martyn Bainbridge
and Ann Curtis

King John	Emrys James	*Essex*	Roger Bizley
Queen Elinor	Hilda Braid	*Fitzwalter*	John Boswall
Prince Henry	Simon Walker	*Bigot*	Philip Dunbar
Blanche of Spain	Louise Jameson	*Beauchamp*	Albert Welling
Philip the Bastard	Richard Pasco	*First Soldier*	John Labanowski
Robert Faulconbrige		*Second Soldier*	Gavin Campbell
	Wilfrid Grove	*Arthur of Brittany*	
Lady Faulconbridge			Benedict Taylor
	Janet Whiteside	*Constance*	Sheila Allen
Hubert	David Suchet	*King Philip of France*	
Salisbury	Denis Holmes		Clement McCallin
Pembroke	Richard Mayes	*Lewis the Dauphin*	Jonathan Kent

Duke of Austria	Gavin Campbell	*Citizen of Angiers*	Leon Tanner
Melun	Ray Armstrong	*Cardinal Pandulph*	Jeffery Dench
Chatillon	Malcolm Armstrong	*Peter of Pomfret*	Mike Gwilym
First French Messenger		*Abbot*	Leon Tanner
	Julian Barnes	*First Monk*	Mike Gwilym
Second French Messenger		*Second Monk*	Michael Ensign
	Mark Cooper		

Aldwych Theatre, London, 1975

Directed by John Barton with Barry Kyle
Designed by John Napier with Martyn Bainbridge
and Ann Curtis

Death, The Presenter	Mike Gwilym	*First Soldier*	John Labanowski
King John	Emrys James	*Second Soldier*	Gavin Campbell
Queen Elinor	Hilda Braid	*Arthur of Brittany*	
Prince Henry	Benedict Taylor		Benedict Taylor
Blanche of Spain	Louise Jameson	*Constance*	Sheila Allen
Philip the Bastard	Ian McKellen	*King Philip of France*	
Robert Faulconbridge			Clement McCallin
	Wilfrid Grove	*Louis the Dauphin*	Jonathan Kent
Lady Faulconbridge		*Duke of Austria*	Gavin Campbell
	Janet Whiteside	*Melun*	Ray Armstrong
Salisbury	Denis Holmes	*Chatillon*	Malcolm Armstrong
Pembroke	Richard Mayes	*Citizen of Angiers*	Leon Tanner
Essex	Roger Bizley	*Boy attendant*	Lloyd Martin
Fitzwalter	John Boswall	*Cardinal Pandulph*	Jeffery Dench
Bigot	Philip Dunbar	*Abbot*	Leon Tanner
Beauchamp	Albert Welling	*Second Monk*	Michael Ensign
Hubert	David Suchet		

BBC Television, 1984

Directed by David Giles
Designed by Chris Pemsel

King John	Leonard Rossiter	*Earl of Pembroke*	Robert Brown
Prince Henry	Rusty Livingstone	*Earl of Salisbury*	John Castle
Prince Arthur	Luc Owen	*Lord Bigot*	John Flint

Hubert de Burgh	John Thaw	*Melun*	John Moreno
Robert Faulconbridge		*Chatillon*	William Whymper
	Edward Hibbert	*Queen Elinor*	Mary Morris
Philip, the Bastard		*Constance*	Claire Bloom
	George Costigan	*Blanch*	Janet Maw
James Gurney	Mike Lewin	*Lady Faulconbridge*	Phyllida Law
Peter of Pomfret	Alan Collins	*French Herald*	Ian Barritt
King Philip of France	Charles Kay	*English Herald*	Carl Oatley
Lewis, the Dauphin	Jonathan Coy	*Citizen of Angiers*	Clifford Parrish
Lymoges, Duke of Austria		*First Executioner*	Ian Brimble
	Gordon Kaye	*English Messenger*	
Cardinal Pandulph			Ronald Chenery
	Richard Wordsworth	*French Messenger*	Tim Brown

The Other Place, Stratford-upon-Avon, 1988

Directed by Deborah Warner
Designed by Sue Blane

King John	Nicholas Woodeson	*Constance*	Susan Engel
Queen Eleanor	Cherry Morris	*King Philip of France*	David Lyon
Prince Henry	Jo James	*Lewis the Dauphin*	Ralph Fiennes
Blanche of Spain	Julia Ford	*Limoges, Archduke of Austria*	
Earl of Pembroke			Darryl Forbes-Dawson
	Richard Bremmer	*Melun*	Patrick Robinson
Earl of Salisbury		*Chatillon*	Roger Watkins
	Edward Harbour	*Hubert*	Robert Demeger
Lord Bigot	Darryl Forbes-Dawson	*Cardinal Pandulph*	Antony Brown
Philip Faulconbridge		*Executioners*	Patrick Robinson
	David Morrissey		Roger Watkins
Robert Faulconbridge	Jo James	*Messenger*	Jo James
Lady Faulconbridge		*Peter of Pomfret*	Roger Watkins
	Denise Armon	*Messenger*	Julia Ford
James Gurney	Patrick Robinson		
Arthur, Duke of Brittany			
	Lyndon Davies		

The Pit, Barbican, London, 1989

Directed by Deborah Warner
Designed by Sue Blane

King John Nicholas Woodeson
Queen Eleanor Cherry Morris
Prince Henry Jack James
Blanche of Spain
Caroline Harding
Earl of Pembroke Richard
Bremmer
Earl of Salisbury
Edward Harbour
Lord Bigot Simon Dormandy
Philip Faulconbridge
David Morrissey
Robert Faulconbridge Jack James
Lady Faulconbridge Cissy Collins
James Gurney Patrick Robinson

Arthur, Duke of Brittany
Nehme Fadlallah
Constance Susan Engel
King Philip of France David Lyon
Lewis the Dauphin Ralph Fiennes
Limoges, Archduke of Austria
Simon Dormandy
Melun Patrick Robinson
Chatillon Roger Watkins
Hubert Robert Demeger
Cardinal Pandulph Julian Curry
Executioners Patrick Robinson
Roger Watkins
Messenger Jack James
Peter of Pomfret Roger Watkins
Messenger Caroline Harding

INDEX